LEADERELIABILITY

Where Leadership, Culture,
and
Profitability Collide

JEFF DUDLEY

iUniverse LLC
Bloomington

LEADERELIABILITY
WHERE LEADERSHIP, CULTURE, AND PROFITABILITY COLLIDE

iUniverse books may be ordered through booksellers or by contacting:

iUniverse
1663 Liberty Drive
Bloomington, IN 47403
www.iuniverse.com
1-800-Authors (1-800-288-4677)

ISBN: 978-1-4917-0169-0 (sc)
ISBN: 978-1-4917-0171-3 (hc)
ISBN: 978-1-4917-0170-6 (e)

Library of Congress Control Number: 2013913888

Printed in the United States of America.

iUniverse rev. date: 8/27/2013

LeadeReliability is derived from an accumulation of my experiences during thirty-two years in the manufacturing sector of industry. My intent is to cause you to think differently about how you do things and to change the way you act based upon that thinking.

Life is an open book that I learn from every day; since leadership is all about sharing what you know with others, I want to pass learning and understanding on to you.

CONTENTS

FOREWORD

The essence of effective leadership is the leader's capacity to enhance the performance and sustainability of the enterprise while engaging stakeholders with a vision and goals infused with hope and opportunity. Further, an effective leader is open to evaluating and adopting techniques and systems to advance his or her leadership agenda.

In *LeadeReliabilty*, Jeff Dudley, a talented leader and enlightened thinker, offers a well-grounded perspective and system that explains how organizations—through effective leadership in the service of a systematic, disciplined focus on reliability—can become more successful and ultimately sustainable.

This book is the product of a leader who—for more than three decades—has practiced what he has preached regarding reliability. As a result, he has generated impressive results that are applicable in a wide variety of settings—from operationally intensive enterprises to more service-oriented ones. *LeadeReliabilty* is eclectic, refreshingly original, practical, organized, and engaging.

I take special pleasure in recommending this book to you. I believe in what Jeff has to say; as his longtime leadership advisor for many years, I have witnessed his personal growth as a leader. I take great delight in his passion for the relationship between leadership and reliability, which he has expressed so well in this book.

May you take pleasure in reading this book and benefit from the rich insights it has in store for you.

Myles Martel, PhD
president and CEO
Martel & Associates
Gulfstream, Florida

INTRODUCTION

Welcome to LeadeReliability, a concept that will allow you to think about how you could do things differently to create a place for yourself or your organization where your results become much different than they are today. It will grow customer loyalty, create employee satisfaction, and allow you to create increased profits and increased margin if you are a business. If you are an individual, it will create time for you to be the person you want to be.

When you wander through the business section, self-help section, or management section of any popular bookstore, you will see many books on the topics of leadership, culture, and how to profitably run a business. But you will be hard-pressed to find any book about the relationship between any two—let alone all three. These three independent factors are essential for your organization to sustain the highest mode of performance. Without all three, your organization will be less than it could be—and you will ultimately disappoint your stakeholders and yourself.

Since all three are critical, I hope to get you to think about the direct and indirect impact all three have on each other. What if you purposefully developed leadership in every person in your organization and created a unique culture that delivered significantly higher profitability? You would be talking about developing a culture of reliability; since leadership is essential to that reliability culture, I call it LeadeReliability.

I have thought about leadership and culture—and how they create profitability—for much of my thirty-two years in the chemical industry, but I have studied it intensely for the past twelve years. My professional experience as a global leader for a large corporation has given me a chance to test these theories and principles.

The culture of reliability is one of the key aspects of allowing your organization to perform at levels that you have never thought possible. Reliability is the answer to many of the problems that are plaguing your organization today. If customer loyalty, employee satisfaction, brand security, recognition, or profitability holds back you or your organization, starting the journey toward LeadeReliability will positively affect any or all of them.

What is reliability—and why is it plaguing you or your organization? Reliability is not an initiative, but it becomes how you do everything that you do.

Initiative is defined as the power or ability to begin; to follow through energetically with a plan or task; determination of a beginning or introductory step; an opening move.

This is where reliability separates itself from the word *initiative*. A first move or something you start to resolve an issue is not my definition of reliability. Starting implies that there is a finish. Beginning suggests that something else will follow. Reliability is different. The fundamental premise is that reliability is not what you do—it is how you do everything.

The journey toward reliability never ends and can always be improved. The start of the journey is just the beginning—and it does not define what reliability is. As reliability develops it will become the way you do everything that you do.

It is not the start of anything or the beginning of something; it is a complete change of how you do everything. It is the way you become. If you are in an organization, then the entire organization changes how they do everything. Regardless of what change you are looking for, if you want to do something differently—or drive an organization to change what it does—it starts with you.

Leadership books talk about what it takes to become a leader, but they never really talk about what it is you are leading. Leadership is an important part of reliability; it is so important that it requires every member of the organization to become a leader. Without leadership, you will never achieve LeadeReliability because it is so completely intertwined with reliability and therefore the name.

Much of what you will read in this book has been influenced by my personal application of these principles as a leader of large, global organizations and the various leadership books I have read. When I read, I search for what makes an individual different from others. I look for concepts and ideas I can use to improve the type of leader I am. I try to apply that new knowledge and refine it as I learn.

Booker T. Washington's *Up From Slavery* taught me to look for the good in all situations and not to allow negative experiences to impact me in negative ways. If you allow someone who has wronged you to negatively affect you, then that person has controlled you and you are no longer controlling yourself.

At Canaan's Edge by Taylor Branch and *Long Walk to Freedom* by Nelson Mandela taught me to be brave and steadfast as a leader and not to allow outside forces—no matter how severe—to force me to stop doing something I believe in. Those books taught me that if I really want to change something dramatically, like a culture, I would always meet severe opposition and that I would have to be stronger than the opposition to succeed. My learnings from the books were validated; I have experienced intense pushback when trying to create a reliability culture. I know firsthand that you can never allow that pushback to cause you to stop.

1864: Lincoln at the Gates of History by Charles Bracelen Flood taught me to work with others to get the success I desire. John Maxwell's *21 Irrefutable Laws of Leadership* is a cookbook of twenty-one traits that a leader must have to be successful. *Good to Great* by Jim Collins taught me to surround myself with a good team, first, to have a chance at success. Never think you have arrived because your competition will pass you by—or you will stop growing. Each of these books contains great nuggets for how to lead and what to do, but the reader needs to apply these nuggets to something. All of them suggest that leaders need to do something to change or improve how they are doing things.

Creating a new culture is a dramatic, dynamic event, and it takes a long time to move from the existing one to the new one. Changing a culture is not an initiative, and it can take years. It is certainly not driven by one event. Changing a culture takes tremendous courage, willingness to deal with opposition, and patience. Cultures do not change overnight, and significant change does not occur until the majority of the participants behave in the new ways. This is where many attempts to change a culture fail.

Throughout history, great leaders who have led cultural change—such as Gandhi, Mandela, Mother Teresa, Lincoln, and Martin Luther King Jr.—held an absolute conviction that the culture needed to be changed, and they would not be swayed from what they believed to be true. When you look at that list of names, think of the opposition they experienced and endured to cause the culture to change. The opposition was constant, but they simply would not back down from the creation of a new, better culture. Because of their leadership, the culture ultimately changed. If you search the web for "culture change," you will see many possibilities for changing a culture. What do you want to change the culture to?

You can also find significant amounts of information about how to run a business successfully. Most discussions center on organization and systems and models. The suggestions include organizational designs or applications of system models that can change the way your business operates—and the amount of profit you will make. While these ideas are important, organizational design is critical for any successful business. The key to any successful enterprise is people—and how they respond to every situation. Have you captured the hearts of your employees? Do they really care about what they are doing and what you want them to do? Are your employees waiting for you to lead them through decisions? Are they applying academic responses to the problems? Truly successful businesses have earned the trust of their employees and stakeholders. With this trust, you can create dedication and allegiance from them.

If you apply what you are about to read in this book, you can predict what the change will look like in the future. That change will include the optimization of resources and more profits (if you are a business).

Now is the time to do something!

CHAPTER 1

WHY RELIABILITY?

Simplicity is a prerequisite for reliability.
—Edsger Dijkstra

Why reliability? I start this book with this question, and I finish this book with the answer. Reliability is not what you do, but it must become how you do everything. It ultimately can provide the answer to many things that are troubling you and your organization. If you don't do everything with a focus on reliability, you will never be consistent in what you do. It is virtually impossible to consistently deliver on your commitments without it becoming how you do everything. Reliability is how you do everything instead of what you do. To create reliability it requires three distinct facets depending on whether you are talking about individual reliability or organizational reliability. However, you can't develop organizational reliability unless you first develop personal reliability within the organization.

PERSONAL

- changing the way you think
- changing the behaviors you perform
- unwavering commitment to learn and to teach

1

Organizational

- development of culture
- leadership by everyone in the organization
- patience and bravery to take on the challenge

In each case, they are interrelated and necessary. Without them, LeadeReliability will fail somewhere along the way. LeadeReliability is where culture, leadership, and profits collide.

What will reliability deliver? Reliability will deliver satisfied customers, completely engaged employees, and significantly better margins. Your business model, products, and services determine your ability to be profitable, but if your model allows it, reliability will maximize that profit. You will maximize your profits, engage your employees, and satisfy your customers if you minimize unplanned events, which is what LeadeReliability focuses on.

Constant and consistent delivery on your commitments is my definition of reliability. You have to do it—and each individual in an organization has to do it. Each group has to do it, each department has to do it, and each function has to do it. Your entire organization has to do it, and that is where leadership comes in. Reliability starts with an individual and spreads to the organization, and as the organization creates reliability, it spreads to each individual. Now you understand why LeadeReliability is so hard. When you do everything with a focus on that constant and consistent delivery of your commitments, the lyrics to a song come true.

It doesn't matter what you've heard
Impossible is not a word.
It's just a reason for someone not to try.[1]

---

[1] Kutless, "What Faith Can Do," *All Is Well: A Worship Album,* 2009.

LeadeReliability is not impossible, but it is not easy either. In the world of integration or isolation, complexity or simplification, cutting-edge or basic, regulation or deregulation, growing or shrinking, expanding or contracting, global or local, multifaceted or straight-lined, broad or narrow, there are not many corporations that can be classified as highly reliable.

Why is it more impossible than easy? We aren't reliable because we have not developed the required individual commitment and culture. We have not insisted that everyone in our organization becomes a leader. Most of all, we are not always brave or patient. If you could develop a culture where everyone leads and develops patience, you would constantly and consistently deliver on your commitments to your customers—and you would differentiate yourself from your competition. You would become unique. You would be different. You would be completely reliable. LeadeReliability would be your culture.

Why LeadeReliability instead of the other movements that we have talked about for decades? For years, corporate initiatives and movements have been designed to deliver customer satisfaction. They focused on the quality of products and the processes that delivered them. Why not just do one of those and do it well?

W. Edwards Deming and his fourteen points set off to transform American industry.[2] By adhering to his fourteen points of production and service, industry would stay in business and protect jobs and investors. In *Good to Great*, Jim Collins shows that this is not necessarily true. Some companies stumbled on their way to success.

Another of Deming's principles was to create consistency of purpose toward improvement of product and service so that customers would always be satisfied. Although many companies adopted all fourteen of the points and made them a way of life,

---

[2]   W. Edwards Deming, *Out of the Crisis: Quality, Productivity, and Competitive Position* (Cambridge: Cambridge University Press, 1982).

they failed to become highly reliable—and some have failed to stay in business.

Total Quality Management is an integrated philosophy for continuously improving the quality of products and processes. Its success works on the premise that everyone in the organization is responsible for the quality of the final product, which they are. However, in many organizations not everyone takes on that responsibility; quality is thought to be solely the responsibility of the quality function. If we engage management, the workforce, and our customers, we should be able to meet and exceed the customers' expectations. The concept is absolutely correct, but few have achieved this state. Very few have constantly and consistently delivered on their commitments.

Joseph Juran was a pioneer in quality in the 1950s.[3] His interests blossomed after his first visit to Japan. He wrote *The Quality Control Handbook* in 1951, and it is now in its sixth printing. Juran created the concept of the Pareto Principle, which separates the "vital few" from the "useful many." Even though millions have followed these principles and steps for quality management, reliability has not been achieved. All these focused on product quality and have been around for decades, but still we don't have LeadeReliability.

At the turn of the century, Six Sigma and Lean technologies became prominent. They focused on expansive toolkits that would deliver permanent solutions to industrial problems, cut waste, and streamline the ability to deliver. Not many companies developed a constant and consistent ability to meet customer expectations and requirements. The concepts described above set the foundation and transformed into Six Sigma and Lean philosophy.

Six Sigma was developed by Motorola in 1986 and is used throughout modern industry. It seeks to remove the defects from the process to minimize the variability of the process. It uses

---

[3]   Juran.com, "Juran: The Source of Quality."

statistics and other methods to minimize errors. Since it deals with statistics and methods, it usually morphs quickly into what you do—rather than *how* you do everything. It becomes a project rather than a way of life.

Lean manufacturing—sometimes referred to as value-stream mapping—attempts to eliminate any actions, behaviors, or steps that do not create value for the end customer. Derived from the Toyota Production System, it is targeted toward preserving value by doing less work. It is a remarkable initiative, but quality issues at Toyota prove it is not always reliable.

Lack of reliability resulted in a loss in consumer confidence as a result of Toyota's 2010 recall, which was the automobile manufacturer's biggest in its seventy-year history. The brand had been synonymous with quality and reliability. What started as an innocuous issue of improperly laid-out mats resulted in a recall of four million vehicles—and was followed by eight million more for sticking accelerator pedals and loss of braking on its Prius, Lexus HS250h, and the Sai models.[4]

Lack of reliability impacts customer confidence and is terribly expensive. Your level of reliability helps create your brand. It takes many actions to create trust, which is an extension of reliability, but it only takes one action to destroy that trust. The Deepwater Horizon oil spill in the Gulf of Mexico had significant negative effects on BP. The spill went on for three months in 2010 and significantly damaged the BP brand.

A single problem can change the perception of a brand overnight. Reliability can offer brand protection—and many other things. The more reliable, trustworthy, and confident those outside your company become in your ability to do whatever you do, the more secure you can become. This even translates to the individual level. We all have a personal brand. Deliver constantly

---

[4] Total Recall: Impact Assessment of Toyota's Quality Issues on Its North American Business," Feb. 17, 2010.

and consistently on your commitments, and your personal brand will be elevated. Reliability can be applied to one individual—or to the largest corporation in the world.

Why choose reliability? Coming to this solution has not been a quick process. It develops over time. I want to save you that time so you can get started on your journey today.

I started my journey in the early nineties and solidified my thinking over the last twenty years. The only way to create a sustainable and highly profitable business that will stand out from its competitors and other corporations is to become highly reliable. Being reliable creates the time and resources that allow you to innovate, which will keep you ahead of the game.

The cornerstone of my belief focused on product quality. I began to develop my thinking about what we did—and *how* we did everything. I thought that if we did everything right the first time, we could satisfy our customers' needs. DRIFT (Doing It Right the First Time) or Zero Defects was pioneered by Philip Crosby in *Quality Is Free*. This philosophy shows how you can achieve high quality in the most economical fashion by reducing the cost of failures. Minimizing the impact of unplanned events is the basis of becoming highly reliable.

The concept of doing it right the first time became the basis of my philosophy and the start of my journey toward LeadeReliability. However, I soon realized that product quality could not be the only focus. Product quality is just a small portion of the total picture. If you want high reliability, it has to go across the organization. Whether it is a small business with a few people or a global corporation with tens of thousands of employees, the formula is the same. You have to create a culture where every person is focused on minimizing the effect of unplanned events and constantly and consistently delivers on his or her commitments. It must become how you hire people, how you sell yourself to customers, how you market yourself to the public, how you schedule your production, and how you pay your bills. It is how you do everything.

Without the concept of reliability being practiced across the entire organization, you will only get incremental improvement. I think it is fair to say that many organizations incrementally improve over time, but few get the quantum improvement that enables them to differentiate their companies. That incremental improvement typically comes in a few areas. For years, companies focused on product quality—and some were successful at improving it. However, if you haven't put that same effort across the entire organization, you may deliver a product that meets customers' needs, but they don't know when they will get it, they don't know if they will be invoiced properly for it, and they don't know how it will be delivered. You may have met their product quality requirements, but your customers would never call you reliable.

Many companies have been audited by external organizations and have received awards and certificates of qualification. J. D. Power and Associates declare which companies are leaders in customer satisfaction, but these same companies struggle with reliability. ISO certifications are handed out to companies who are, by definition, practicing good quality management, but many are not reliable. If all these initiatives are out there—and companies can even be audited to be labeled as practicing good quality management—why aren't many companies or corporations constantly and consistently meeting their commitments? It is hard work to get an entire organization to act like leaders. It is hard work for a company or corporation to be patient. It is hard work to create a culture that looks at reliability as how you do everything rather than just another thing to do.

The journey toward creating a reliability culture is a long one, and it is not for the faint of heart. Like any cultural journey, it will not come easy—and it will not be without its moments where you might believe it is just too hard or that results will never come.

Although it is a hard journey, the rewards so greatly outweigh the effort that it is well worth taking. Those brave and diligent enough to create a culture where all people consistently and constantly meet their commitments will differentiate themselves from everyone else.

The dynamic of reliability is an interesting one because it is completely different from any other undertaking your organization has attempted. Reliability contains many of the parts of other initiatives that are described above, but the development of a LeadeReliability culture is much different than anything the organization has done before. The creation of this way of being or doing work is not an initiative or a program—it is the way you do everything for the rest of your life. As an individual, it will transform more than what you are working on. If you are working on it in your organization, it will transform your professional life and your personal life. If it is undertaken and created this way, it will not fade or die like so many other initiatives and programs have. It will change your life forever.

Why reliability? Why *not* reliability? It will change how you do everything.

CHAPTER 2

SOUNDS SO SIMPLE!
WHAT MAKES IT SO HARD?

Life is either a daring adventure or nothing.
—Helen Keller

Conceptually, keeping our commitments seems pretty simple. All we have to do is do what we say we are going to do—and then we are considered reliable. Doing this is much easier said than done. What makes personal reliability so hard? Why can't people constantly and consistently keep their commitments? In order for an individual to become reliable, he or she must practice minimizing the impact of unplanned events. Over the years, I have surveyed individuals and discovered that most people waste forty or more days of their year managing unplanned events. Forty days! People lose more than a month of their year managing unplanned events. What makes up those unplanned events? It is mostly little things.

If you get in your car one morning and it doesn't start, you are unable to leave for whatever you had planned to do. How much of the rest of your day will be consumed by dealing with the car that doesn't start? How can you minimize the impact this unplanned event? Was your car telling you it was about to have a problem? Was it harder to start your car recently? Was it making an odd sound that you failed to pay attention to? Was it leaking something that you ignored? Are you a driver who doesn't pay attention to those gauges and noises in your car? Cars are just supposed to work.

You can see how an event can be completely disruptive, but you also have a glimpse of how the impact might be minimized. Now extrapolate this one incident to all the incidents that happen to you at home and work over the course of a day, a week, or a year—and you will see the magnitude of the picture. You might be saying forty days; I am probably closer to eighty. There goes January, February, and some of March!

Imagine getting to work fifteen minutes early because you blocked off your entire morning to work on an upcoming presentation and are anxious to get started. You get a cup a coffee and settle in, but the phone rings just as you log on to your computer. One of your most important customers did not receive the shipment they were expecting the day before—and their manufacturing operation will shut down that afternoon if they don't receive it. How much of your morning will be spent preparing for that presentation? You are the client's salesperson. You don't make the product, store the product, or deliver the product, but you are the face of the company for the customer. Unplanned events are disruptive, and they waste your valuable time and resources. Your morning has now been disrupted—and you don't know for how long.

These are just a few examples of how unplanned events can be disruptive. Apply that to a group of people and multiply the impact; becoming reliable seems impossible. Remember the lyrics to our impossible song? Even though it feels like things are out of your control, there is a pretty good reason to try. To get an entire organization engaged in LeadeReliability, each individual has to work on his or her own reliability. That can be very hard.

- Individuals will choose to engage in reliability. If they don't, the chances for organizational reliability are diminished.
- Each individual has to figure out why he or she cares about reliability *before* he or she engages.

If you have an organization of just three people and one of those people chooses not to engage, that person will not constantly and consistently deliver on his or her commitments. What will the other two people have to do to compensate? They will have to work harder and longer, and they will have to cover for the reliability flaws of the other person. Something else happens as well. Overtime, although never stated, those two people will develop a poor opinion of the third person. They will marginalize the person in many aspects and will stop seeking that person's opinions. Even if that unreliable person comes up with the most brilliant idea that could transcend and change the whole organization, there is little chance of it going forward because the person has been marginalized by the others. The chance of this organization achieving LeadeReliability is not very good.

Let's look at the three people in that organization. Two people have to work more to compensate for the problems that are created by the unreliable person. What's their attitude? What's their psychology? They look down on the third person and become frustrated with him or her. Let's look at the unreliable person and his or her perceptions. Whether he or she states it publicly or not, they know they have been marginalized. They know they are not respected. They know their opinions aren't considered. What are his or her feelings? They feel degraded. In this organization, no one is happy—and the organization does not perform at the level that it could because that one member has not adapted reliable behaviors.

Let's take the same situation with three highly reliable people. This group does not have to deal with the issue of unreliability.

This organization would become so reliable that if the service or product they offer is something that is desired by their customers, they would grow and become as profitable as they possibly could. LeadeReliability would deliver customer satisfaction and optimum profitability. In the first situation, unless the unreliable situation was addressed, the organization would struggle with customer satisfaction and profits. It could ultimately go out of business.

Although reliability is typically described as an organizational concept, it's an individual concept that is extrapolated into an organization. Therefore, the necessity for every individual in the organization to deliver LeadeReliability is essential—or the weak link could cause the organization to fail.

The cultural and psychological importance of LeadeReliability is important on a daily basis. When LeadeReliability is achieved, the entire culture minimizes the impact of unplanned events. Although some unplanned events still happen, they are noticed and mitigated at the earliest possible moment. As a result, the entire organization constantly and consistently delivers on their commitments—to each other and to customers.

How does a person who is acting unreliably negatively impact the entire outcome? All unplanned events start small and then escalate. Participants in LeadeReliability anticipate these occurrences and proactively look for them to occur. They are actively looking for obvious signs that something is starting to happen—and then they act. Their actions proactively intervene in the occurrence, and they mitigate the negative outcome. People who are not engaged in this don't notice or don't act, and the unplanned event will get worse. This person's failure to act will delay the response, and he or she depends on someone to notice and take action. When the second person notices and reacts, it may be too late to prevent a negative outcome for the organization. This person will be minimizing the impact of the unplanned event, but not to the degree that the first person could have. You can see why everyone has to be involved.

What is the remedy for people who do not become reliable? Each member of the organization has a choice to act reliably or not. The organization must offer training in these principles, which I describe later. Assuming the training is offered and people are made aware of the need to be reliable, they must choose to become reliable. If they don't, they must leave. If they do not become reliable, they could be the cause of the issues described above. If each individual chooses to engage, that individual decision made multiple times across the organization blossoms into an organization capable of LeadeReliability. Individual engagement in reliability drives the organization. What will make an individual decide?

Each person needs to develop a personal reason to care about reliability, and this is where the organization begins to take over. Why does your organization exist and why does it do what it does? What you do and how you do it matter, but why do you do what you do? That is what captures the heart. *What* and *how* are the academic reasons to minimize unplanned events. There is not one person who will say, "We should have more unplanned events," but not every person can tell you why. Unless you can describe why, then there is no passion and no heart. Unless you have passion and heart, you won't change the culture. You will remain satisfied with the one you are in. Developing *why* is part of the reason culture change is hard. Organizations are typically not good at defining the *why*, but each individual cares about certain things. Uncovering why each person would want to care about reliability begins to move the culture, but it is also what makes it so hard.

Now let's talk more about the organization. I see three difficult issues that cause reliability not to be a focus for an organization.

- Most organizations are tolerant of unplanned events. They are considered normal.

13

- Organizations don't stand by themselves; they are typically highly integrated.
- The organizational *why* is not always defined or understood.

UNPLANNED EVENTS ARE CONSIDERED NORMAL.

Most organizations are tolerant of reoccurring unplanned events. Organizations expect unplanned events to happen, and they build in mechanisms to deal with them, but they seldom build in ways to eliminate them. It is accepted that unplanned events occur, and there is thought to be nothing that can be done about them. Unplanned events are thought to be normal occurrences in business. Executive leaders often use them to explain poor performance or at least the reason why performance was not what it could have been. In Apache Corporation's fourth quarter 2012 earnings call, chairman and CEO, G. Steven Ferris said, "Apache achieved some new milestones in 2012, and first of all, despite significant downtime we grew our annual production ... which is a new record for Apache, and as a matter of information and I assure you not an excuse, I would like to point out had we not experienced the downtime in the North Sea and Hurricane Isaac in the Gulf of Mexico during just the third quarter. Our production would have been 6.3 percent." When you look at Mr. Ferris's statement, he says despite significant downtime we set new milestones. What if they had been more LeadeReliable and did not have the significant downtime? Just imagine what those milestones could have been. Unplanned events can never be considered an explanation for anything, if they are not considered normal.

Unplanned events don't have to be considered normal.

Here is my favorite example. What is the largest department at a car dealership? The answer is the service department. What is the purpose of the service department? The purpose is to proactively repair vehicles in the case of individual drivers who practice some level of reliability and to fix vehicles when they fail. They fail because of the car manufacturer's unreliability or the owner's unwillingness to practice reliable behaviors. Without a doubt, the manufacturer is sometimes responsible for the reliability problems.[5] However, sometimes the blame for the problem can be shared by the manufacturer and the owner. Undetected or ignored unplanned events can be severe.[6] Every year, missing or damaged gas caps cause 147 million gallons of gas to evaporate. This translates to roughly a half a billion dollars that just disappears. Now you understand the significant cost of unreliability.

---

[5]   The majority of the five most common failures and fixes in the index are related to durability instead of faulty parts, supporting industry statistics that consumers are holding on to cars longer and manufacturers are making vehicles to last longer. The data also demonstrates that durable parts, which should last longer, are failing more frequently due to lack of maintenance. As vehicles age, the index repeatedly illustrates the impact of maintenance on gas mileage, safety, the environment, and costs. Ignoring small problems is fueling more expensive repairs. (CarMD.com 2010 Vehicle Health Index, 5 Most Common Failures)

[6]   From 1996 to 2009, loose, missing, or damaged gas caps was the top reason for "check engine-related" repairs. Bumped to No. 2 in 2010, loose, damaged, or missing gas caps cause 147 million gallons of gas to evaporate each year. (CarMD.com 2010 Vehicle Health Index, 5 Most Common Failures)

Make integration more reliable.

We cause much of our own unreliability, but it is an area we can positively impact. Our organizations are not isolated, and our reliability is dependent on other organizations. Most organizations are highly integrated into other organizations and are dependent on their reliability to deliver their own reliability.

We all have had bad experiences with our suppliers and—as a result—have disappointed our customers. The typical mindset is to try to blame the supplier and communicate that to our customers. We share with the customer how our supplier let us down so we couldn't meet their needs. Do you think your customer really cares why you failed? All they know is you did not meet their needs. They don't want excuses; they want their product or service in a constant and consistent fashion. They want you to be reliable. Why don't you become proactive and invest in your supplier's reliability so their ability to supply your needs is not one of your reliability flaws.

What if you develop LeadeReliability—but your suppliers don't? We live a globally integrated world; the combination of most businesses carrying lower inventories and the expectancy of on-time deliveries at short notice makes the reliability of your suppliers paramount to your success. How can you change the way you think about your suppliers so they add to your reliability?

Become reliable yourself.

Without a doubt, the most important thing you can do to increase your suppliers' reliability is to become more reliable yourself. The more predictable you become, the more your suppliers can plan on meeting your needs. If you can forecast your demand, which you can only do if you are highly reliable in all areas of your business, then you can project to your suppliers what you will need from them. You reliability is not just reliable manufacturing. Your reliability depends on a reliable commercial, research-and-development, and purchasing organization. It depends on an organization in which every facet becomes reliable and develops into LeadeReliability.

DIVERSIFY YOUR SUPPLY POSITION.

Resilience or the ability to react quickly to mitigate issues when something goes wrong is one of the most important behaviors to become proficient in. The ability to expect the unexpected and be prepared to respond proactively is vital to success. Where possible, create dual supply sourcing for parts and raw materials. If it is unrealistic for you to have a dual supply, then ensure that some level of supply inventory (critical raw materials, parts, and equipment) is stored at an alternate location and an active emergency plan is in place so you can access the supply quickly.

EDUCATE YOUR SUPPLIERS ON THE IMPORTANCE OF THEIR RELIABILITY.

Some suppliers have not progressed to the point where they think about LeadeReliability. You need to educate them on the importance of their supply to you and how it is imperative that they too become very dependable. If a key supplier of yours is not reliable—and you can't depend on them to deliver what you need—they will, at some point, negatively impact your reliability and ultimately your customer. They may impact you to the point that your reputation is severely damaged with your customers. The more you can educate your supplier about the importance of their reliability, the better off you will be.

Create incentive for your supplier to be reliable.

As we have discussed, it is not easy to become highly reliable. High reliability requires patience and bravery. You need patience because it takes time to get through each stage as you transform your culture through the various stages of reliability. It is essentially impossible to skip steps as you navigate through the reliability stages. Each stage requires some time. We will discuss this more in the future.

The amount of time varies, depending on your organization, but it never can be skipped. By bravery, I mean you will need to have important conversations with your supplier. Sometimes these conversations will be difficult and require you to openly share your disappointment or concerns with them. Also, create a relationship where they can openly share their concerns with you.

These conversations should not be looked at negatively. These types of conversations allow learning to occur from each other—and teach people how to become more reliable. Ultimately they expedite progress through the cultural journey. A way to get your supplier involved is to incentivize their reliability. It will give them a reason to consider the journey. Possibly give more business to the supplier as they become more reliable. Consider giving them exclusivity as long as they guarantee supply, while assuring yourself that you have safeguards in place that cover you if resilience is needed. These are just a few of the ways to incentivize your supplier to become more reliable.

Admit your mistakes and develop a true partnership.

Just like your suppliers, you aren't perfect either. There are times when you provide them wrong or untimely information that may cause waste or issues in their system. Admit your mistakes to them and attempt to understand how your actions can have a negative effect on them. It will create a forum for open communication, and it will let them know you care about their success. Your open communication will allow them to take all your other communications in a different light. If you are open with the negative, they will also give more credence to your positive communications. When you really have a need for something, they will respond more favorably.

TEACH YOUR SUPPLIERS HOW THEY CAN BECOME MORE RELIABLE.

As you learn how to become more reliable, share that learning with your supplier. In an integrated supply chain, you are dependent on their reliability. Without the ability to count on them, your own reliability is at risk. The more you learn about becoming reliable, the more you can teach your supplier. And the more they practice what you teach, the more secure your position of reliability becomes. This may enhance your relationship and partnership with them—and they could treat you differently than others.

DEVELOP TRUST WITH YOUR SUPPLIERS.

All the previous actions will promote and develop trust with your suppliers because these actions create credibility. In *Speed of Trust,* Stephen M. R. Covey states that credibility is the foundation of trust. All actions with your suppliers should work toward establishing this credibility. We have to be transparent with them and offer them good information so they can respond to our needs. We have to create the best chance for them to be successful in serving us. They will desire to work with you if you do this. When you call, you want them to be excited to see how they can help you. Trust is created through your reliability—in the same way that your trust in them is created through their reliability.

Why spend all this time working on reliability with your suppliers? The reason is simple. Your customers depend on your reliability. You are a supplier to them. Without your ability to constantly and consistently meet your customers' needs, they will have limited confidence in you. They will be looking somewhere else to gain that confidence. That will hurt your business. Help your business by investing in the reliability of your suppliers.

MOST ORGANIZATIONS CAN'T TELL YOU *WHY*.

There are many organizations that can tell you what they do and how they do it, but they really can't tell you *why*. If they can't express why they do what they do, then it will be hard to capture the hearts of customers and their employees. Nike doesn't spend any time telling you how they make shoes or even what they make, but they do spend a large portion of their time telling you *why*. "Just do it" is a phrase that consumers can relate to; as a result, the Swoosh captures hearts.

"The Few, the Proud, the Marines" stirs many a heart to join this branch of the service. They don't tell you what they do or how they do it, but you sense the pride in being a marine. Mazda doesn't tell you all about what they do, but the "Zoom-Zoom" in the child's voice might make you go look at one. Why do you do what you do? As an organization, you need to figure that out so that your customers and employees can use it as a basis for their own *why*. Give your employees a reason to care, and they will capture your customers' hearts with the way they do their work.

You now have a glimpse of why creating LeadeReliability is so difficult. How do I know it is difficult? There aren't many organizations that are LeadeReliable. Turning impossible into reality is very hard work. No matter your industry, service, or product, creating LeadeReliability will differentiate you from your competitors.

As a result, customers will desire you—and employees will want to work for you. You will create high customer loyalty and deep employee satisfaction.

CHAPTER 3

VALUE CASE FOR RELIABILITY

The successful person makes a habit of doing
what the failing person doesn't.
—Thomas Edison

There are many reasons why people decide reliability is not for them. Most of those reasons are as credible as an urban legend and prove to be false once you dig into them.

- Being reliable increases your costs.
- If it is not done correctly, you can always redo it, which is cheaper than wasting the time to make it right the first time.
- If you want to be highly productive, you can't be reliable too. It slows you down.
- Cutting costs is the best way to increase margins in tough economic times.
- Make it fast—and then just make sure you have good quality checks to keep customers happy. Inspection after the fact is more cost effective than building reliability into the system.
- People who get you out of a crisis in the eleventh hour are worth their weight in gold.

This is quite a list; if any of these are true, then investing in LeadeReliability is a waste of time and resources—and it will reduce your profits and margins. We should decide if there is really a value case for reliability. Is reliability a cost or an investment? Let's take a look at some of these urban legends and dissect them to see if they are true.

Do it right or redo it?

Can you have a cost advantage by redoing something instead of doing it flawlessly the first time?

Every time I think about this I wonder if someone could go stand in front of mirror and honestly say to himself or herself, "I don't have time to do it right, but I have time to do it again."

Any manufacturing or service work process or procedure is designed to deliver whatever you are making or supplying correctly. It is designed with the intent of doing it correctly so the product or service can be sold to a customer who is willing to buy it. As soon as it ends up wrong, something has become abnormal. The way you did it, what you did it with it, or the customer's expectations have changed—but something has changed. What you intended to do did not work; as a result, you are left with an unsalable product, a deficient service, off-grade material or service, inventory you can't use, or unsatisfied customers. Let's not generalize; let's provide a concrete example to see if you can save money by redoing something.

A manufacturing facility takes one minute to produce a piece. That piece costs three dollars to make, including raw materials, equipment involvement, labor, and other direct production costs. For simplicity's sake, let's say this is the rest of the economics for the manufacturing process:

	$ /production piece
Raw Material	1.00
Labor	1.00
All other direct costs	1.00
Cost to discard piece	4.00 ($3 lost production cost plus $1 disposal)
Cost to rework piece	1.50
Good piece sale price	5.00
Operating rate	1 piece/min

What can you tell from these numbers? If a production piece is made correctly and sold, it creates a profit margin of two dollars. It also appears that if something is wrong with the production, there are two choices. It can possibly be reworked, but if it must be discarded, there is a three-dollar manufacturing cost and an additional dollar disposal cost.

Again for simplicity's sake, let's say everything that can be made can be sold, and this production facility is the market leader for the product. Since the facility is sold out and can produce everything that is made, most managers would be reluctant to shut down the facility because any effort to become more reliable that includes downtime will cause an immediate loss of profits and margin.

If you were the manager of this production line, what would you do?

If the line runs completely reliably, you will make revenue of three hundred dollars per hour and an operation margin of one hundred and twenty dollars. The only way to increase revenue and margin is to increase production throughput, reduce costs, or increase the price. As we have established before, most production and service organizations aren't LeadeReliable. Let's assume that your process runs at a high level of consistency, and 90 percent of everything you make is made correctly the first time. Of the 10 percent that is not, one in six pieces has to be discarded, and the other five can be reworked at a rate of four per hour.

Here are the economics of your production line after an hour at 90 percent reliability:

60 parts have been made

54 parts are ready to sell—revenue of $270 and operating margin of $108

4 parts cost you $6.00 to rework and are ready to sell—revenue $20 and operating margin of $2

1 part is in inventory, waiting to be reworked, so you have $3 of production cost tie-up

1 part has to be discarded at a cost of $4

Here is your balance sheet:

Total revenue (product) $270

Total revenue (rework) $20

Total operating cost $180

Total rework cost $6

Total disposal cost $1

Total revenue after one hour $290

Total operating cost $187

Total operating margin $103

Cost of inventory $3

Since the market is in a sold-out condition, your lack of reliability (the production line operation did not constantly and consistently meet its promise of making good production pieces) reduced your revenue by $10—but it reduced your margin by $17. Extrapolate that to thirty days of operation, and you have lost $12,240 in margin because you are only 90 percent reliable.

Your technical staff has uncovered the problem, and they suggest shutting down for two days to increase the reliability of production to 95 percent by making some adjustments on the production line. What would your response be?

You have two choices now that this option has been presented.

"We can't shut down because we are sold out—and if we do, we will lose too much revenue" or "We start the modifications today, but I am counting on your individual reliability so that when we resume production, I am expecting the production line to operate at 95 percent reliability."

If the production line runs at 95 percent reliability, the economic outcome of the line will look like this after one hour:

60 parts get made

57 parts are ready to sell—revenue of $285 and operating margin of $114

3 parts cost you $4.50 to rework and are ready to sell—revenue is $15 and the operating margin is $1.50

0 parts are in inventory waiting to be reworked

1 part has to be discarded at a cost of $2 (one part every two hours)

Here is your balance sheet:

Total revenue (product) $285

Total revenue (rework) $15

Total operating cost $180

Total rework cost $4.50

Total disposal cost $.50 (one part every two hours)

Total revenue after one hour of operation $300

Total operating cost $185

Total operating margin $115

Cost of inventory $0

If you do the economics, running at 95 percent does a few things to brighten the fiscal picture. Your revenue will increase by $10 to $300, and your operating margin will increase to $115 or $12 per hour. Your rework revenue will go down, but now you will only discard one piece every two hours instead of every hour—and you will build up no inventory of rework pieces.

With these improved economics, if you had to shut down for two days to make the repairs and they were reliable, your margin loss would be $4,944 for those two days of missed operations at 90 percent reliability. You would compensate for your downtime in roughly 16.5 days. On day seventeen, you would be making $288 more per day.

In May, you run at 90 percent reliability. On June 15, you get brave, make the reliability repair, and shut down for two days. Everyone says, "We must be crazy to shut down because we are sold out." However, from July on, people will change their point of view. They will think shutting down was a work of genius—and it is all due to increased reliability.

Month	Revenue	Margin	Comments
May	$215,760	$76,632	Running at 90 percent reliability, sold out
June	$198,800	$74,760	Two-day downtime to improve reliability
July	$223,200	$85,500	Reliability improvement + 5 percent = margin +12 percent

Fallacy: You can create a cost advantage by redoing something, rather than doing it flawlessly the first time.

Fact: Reliability creates margin expansion and is always an investment.

No matter what your margin, there will be some point in time when making the brave decision toward becoming more reliable will ultimately increase your margins. Reliability is always an investment that you must decide whether you are willing to make.

Who are your most valuable employees?

What type of employee is more valuable to you—one who corrects the crisis or one who prevents it from ever happening? My friend was an acquaintance of Jean Kirkpatrick, a former ambassador to the United Nations. She once made the statement that a good statesperson was one who prevented something bad from happening—and nobody knew about it. That statement rings true for reliability. This is not so true in most of today's corporate world.

Which employees get all the notoriety and praise? The ones who arrive after the crisis and get things back in order. It is not usually those who see the early signs that a crisis could occur and prevent it from getting worse. Hollywood loves the hero who arrives just in the nick of time to prevent the disaster from getting worse. There aren't too many top-selling movies about the person who prevented the disaster from ever starting. However, they are the true heroes.

Going back to our example in the first fallacy, who do you think will get the ultimate glory for the 5 percent increase in reliability? Most likely, it will be those who figured out what the problem was and created the case for making the changes that would increase the reliability. I am not saying they don't deserve credit for doing a good job and figuring it out, but in my opinion, depending on the circumstance, that is what technical staffs are paid to do. The real question is what took them so long. Although we don't know the history of the 90 percent reliability, before we reward those involved, we should consider how the operation got to 90 percent reliability.

If the 90 percent operating reliability is an increase from a previously lower reliability—and the facility is incrementally improving in reliability—then I applaud the efforts of the organization. This assumes that the technical group confirmed they had a solution and brought it forward for a decision on the same day. Any delay in taking the idea forward would delay the opportunity to increase the margin in the future by the amount described above. This would be the best case and describes an organization working on LeadeReliability.

What if the line was brought up at its designed rate originally, which was much higher than 90 percent reliability, but gradually degraded in reliability over time? The degradation occurred gradually enough that the change went unnoticed—until someone began to investigate the line's performance and discovered they were no longer running at design rates. In this scenario, the change went unnoticed for too long. If someone had been watching the situation closely, the reliability would never have slipped.

The reward system in this type of organization is often partially to blame. Those who prevent degradation from occurring through constant attention often have their efforts go unnoticed. And those who come in after the fact and offer solutions are often treated like heroes. In these organizations, the occurrence of unplanned events is treated as normal. In the organization where preventing the incidents from occurring is the rewarded behavior, you tend to see abnormal quickly identified and corrected before it becomes an issue.

The two most likely scenarios have been described. Which employee's behavior creates the most profit? It will always be the one who proactively prevents anything negative from occurring because they quickly react to the slightest changes. Why aren't these people the heroes? Those who come to action after the crisis are simply doing their jobs. Most organizations don't constantly and consistently look to minimize the impact of unplanned events. They wait for them to happen and then attempt to address them. Anyone with the proper skills can work to solve a problem—no matter how difficult. It takes a special mind-set to catch things early so the unplanned event doesn't cause problems.

In our example above, if the reliability had degraded over time, had someone been acting in a LeadeReliable manner and prevented it from drifting the whole way to 90 percent, each day it had been not allowed to fade would have be a day of increased margin. In the best case, if the machine had always run at design rate, it would have meant someone was looking for any small deviation from normal on a continuous basis and was responding to it. Imagine the money that would have been made.

Fallacy: The employee who corrects a problem after the crisis has occurred is your most valuable employee.

Fact: The proactive employee who detects issues and solves them before they develop into problems is your most valuable employee.

If an organization is proactively looking for abnormal and reacting to solve the issue once it is detected, it will create much more profit than an organization that waits for the problem to occur and then attempts to address it.

Are you reliable enough?

Many people say, "We are already reliable enough. I don't need to be more reliable."

You may be correct. Your present system may allow you to meet your customers' needs on a continuous basis, but if you have not developed LeadeReliability, you are not extracting all the value you can out of the service you provide or product you produce. You are leaving significant profit on the table. My studies of a number of organizations say that if you have never thought about LeadeReliability, you are continuing to operate the way you always have, are not constantly and consistently delivering on your commitments, and are not minimizing the impact of unplanned events. Approximately 10 percent[7] of your revenue stream is being used to compensate for unplanned events, and about 15 percent[8] of your resources are spending their time dealing with these unplanned events. This is a significant expenditure that does not need to be wasted. It is time and resources that an organization can't afford to waste. What would you do with 10 percent more revenue? It could be invested, used for expansion, spent on research and development, or used to reward employees. With 10 percent more revenue, you could simply take that much more profit. The opportunities are endless—but only if you focus on LeadeReliability. If your company, business, or organization could use more profits and resources, then start the journey to LeadeReliability.

Fallacy: We are already reliable enough; I don't need to be more reliable.

Fact: You can always be more reliable, and it will always deliver you more profit and better utilization of your resources.

The LeadeReliability journey is the classic "peeling of the onion." Once you start, you will never be satisfied. Unplanned events that you are working on this year would not have been on your radar screen last year. You will continue to refine your operations and sharpen your perspective. You will become intolerant of unplanned events, and you will detect their occurrence earlier because you will have the time and resources to focus on them.

---

[7]   This figure is based on personal experience and benchmarking in various industries and organizations.

[8]   Through benchmarking and surveys, the amount of time spent dealing with unplanned events can be determined. This is based on personal benchmarking conducted with over 2500 individuals, globally, who were from different organizational functions.

We have a great quality department—so I don't need reliability. Can a robust after-the-fact quality system be more cost effective than a LeadeReliable culture?

I am sure many organizations have brilliant quality organizations and do a great job physically and statistically to assure that the correct amount of quality assurance and control is being applied to the product. Many of the outside agency-regulated (pharmaceuticals as an example) or customer-regulated (electronics as an example) businesses have made this the solution to delivering quality products. However, no matter how good the programs and systems are, unless you have the capability to do 100 percent testing, you can't completely assure the quality of the product. Using a quality department to ensure the degree to which you can assure quality is very expensive. I worked for a while with a biopharmaceutical business, and we essentially had one quality person for every operations person. We had one person making the product—and one person making sure the operations person was doing his or her job. Any satisfaction the customer experiences from this type of system comes with a heavy burden on the organization and a heavy price. Can you achieve the same result another way? I think the answer is yes.

What if every person in the organization takes the responsibility to constantly and consistently deliver on the promise the company makes to the customer? What if every person in the organization takes the personal responsibility to minimize the impact of unplanned events? What if all individuals in the organization have a reason to care about how they perform their jobs and desire to completely please the customers? You are now talking about an organization that is working toward LeadeReliability. The advantage to this approach is that it will be done at a much lower cost and with much better results.

Let's look at the dynamics of an organization that depends on its quality control and assurance as separate functions from operations to ensure quality versus a culture that is LeadeReliable across the organization.

When an organization puts in an entire function that is assigned to control and assure quality, especially one of significant size and influence, it becomes easy to rationalize that quality is their focus and their job. I have seen the functions of quality and operations develop into an adversarial relationship in which each is trying to influence the other. I have seen this develop to the degree that one sometimes wonders if they are working in the same direction. Many times, this dynamic drives the operations organization to work on getting the product made, and the quality organization works on making sure the product was made "good." When the "goodness" of the product comes into question, typically the operations group becomes defensive and questions the validity of the quality test. They often ask for a reevaluation of the quality of the product to confirm the "goodness" test. What message is being sent? Not that the product is possibly off quality, but that the quality organization made a mistake. When the "goodness" of a product is deemed acceptable, we never recheck it to confirm that fact.

Automatically, the premise established by operations is that there is a good chance the quality test is wrong because what they do often comes into question. In this situation, it is easy to see how two groups supposedly working for the same outcome can develop an adversarial relationship that becomes more about the power of the organization than the product being delivered to the customer.

Setting up a separate department to monitor quality control and quality assurance is also very costly. For instance, producing pharmaceuticals is a costly endeavor for many reasons, but if there is one quality person for every operations person, extensive quality control and assurance departments will add to the cost. In certain industries, the cost of poor quality has such a negative

---

impact that the extra cost is worth it. That may be the case, but what if you took a different approach to ensure the quality?

What if all people in the organization felt the ultimate responsibility for the quality of the process and the product? What if it didn't matter what department they worked in, they knew it was their job to produce and ensure a quality product for the customer. What if they were positively rewarded for noticing any flaw that would prevent that from happening? In this case, the operations workers would also be part of quality control and quality assurance. They would know they were responsible for making product—and making a "good" product. They would constantly be looking for flaws and trying to detect them as early as possible to correct the problems. There would be no questioning quality tests or checks because the employees making the product would also be testing the product for "goodness." The staffing level would be optimum to ensure that the quality of the product was assured and controlled—but not to the excess described above. Everyone in the organization would be about fixing the problem—not one group trying to catch the problems that another group caused.

Fallacy: We have a top-notch quality organization. Quality control and quality assurance allow our customers to be guaranteed satisfaction.

Fact: Making everyone responsible for the quality control and quality assurance of the product is more efficient and will have long-lasting results.

The key to creating LeadeReliability is the complete involvement of every individual in the organization. The task is to minimize the impact of unplanned events. It is not a particular group's job to monitor one area and another's to monitor another area. When they do, they create silos—and people only worry about *their* jobs. In LeadeReliability, people have key areas of focus, but they are encouraged to identify and address any situation that looks like the beginning of an unplanned event.

We have developed an arguable position against some of the common beliefs and urban legends that would cause someone to argue against reliability. There are others that exist, but they prove to be invalid when analyzed. These brief descriptions allow you to see how LeadeReliability moves the economic needle to the positive. Increased profits, although important, are not the only driver. This type of organization, while definitely increasing profits, also offers brand protection, sustainability, employee satisfaction, and increased customer loyalty. Your customers will develop a loyalty so strong that they will often become your strongest advocates. As you constantly and consistently meet your customer expectations, they become more than customers, they become allies.

The final economic justification for LeadeReliability is that it makes sense no matter what the external economic headwinds look like. When the economy has strong tailwinds and is advancing, LeadeReliability creates customer trust and loyalty, increases your margins, and allows you to supply constantly and consistently at maximum capacities. When the winds turn against you and the economy is in a downturn, LeadeReliability allows you to maximize the impact of your valuable resources. You will not be wasting your resources on unplanned events—you will be using those resources to continue to develop customer loyalty and margin optimization.

Now you have proof that reliability is always an investment and never a cost.

CHAPTER 4

RELIABILITY REQUIRES
A MIND-SET

Life is not about finding yourself.
Life is about creating yourself.
—George Bernard Shaw

Does your organization have a mind-set that allows you to be reliable enough to do what you are doing today or do you have an organizational mind-set to be as reliable as you could be? These two mind-sets are different. Being only reliable enough will get you average performance. Being as reliable as you could be will deliver much more to you, your employees, and your customers.

Becoming as reliable as you could be will improve customer loyalty, increase employee engagement, and increase your profits and margins.

What is the definition of reliability? The dictionary defines reliability as "capable of being trustworthy" and offers "responsible" as a synonym. My definition goes a little deeper. With my definition of reliability (LeadeReliability), we are talking about the constant and consistent ability to meet your commitments to your customers, stakeholders, and employees. Constant means all the time, and consistent means every person in your organization.

With that definition, if you said you are as reliable as you could be, it would mean that every person in your organization—on an hourly, daily, weekly, monthly, and annual basis—maintains the mind-set to allow reliability to constantly and consistently deliver a reason for customer loyalty, a desire for employee engagement, and increasing shareholder value.

Constant and consistent performance requires unwavering behavior. As with any behavior, you can create the drive for this unwavering behavior by adopting it yourself—which is usually the most effective—or someone else can create it for you. The reason behind the drive to faithfully and uniformly carry out the behavior has to be so compelling that you can't afford not to follow it. Something has to make performing it so positive—or not performing it so negative—that you and the organization won't risk taking a shortcut. When an organization performs at this level, customers and clients view them as LeadeReliable. They are completely trustworthy, and the expectations of everyone involved—individual, organization, and customer—are met. Yet there aren't many organizations that meet this high standard of internal operation and external delivery. Here are some thoughts on why this might be the case.

For the last fifteen years I have studied industries that have achieved a high level of LeadeReliability—pharmaceutical, aviation, military, and nuclear. I am convinced the success of these organizations can be credited to the existence of a compelling reason for them to become more reliable. In each case, the compelling reason is some form of regulatory obligation. I am not an advocate of regulatory agencies dictating what organizations should or shouldn't do, and I am not in favor of government control. I just find it interesting that organizations that must perform to some degree of regulatory scrutiny realize they must be reliable or face negative consequences. As a result, they are often able to do it profitably. What does regulation create—and would it be possible to reap the same positive benefits without having to be held to external regulations? In short, how can an organization regulate itself?

Regulation creates a platform that ensures the end state of the product or service—and the methods to produce or deliver it are at a level that meets essential parameters. As a result, the product or service can be safely consumed or used by the customer. The entire organization is held accountable to these regulations and must perform their roles to meet them. Organizations in these regulated industries have no choice but to consistently and constantly deliver—or they will be forced out of business, fined, or both. That is what regulation creates on the service and product side. However, if the organization is privately held, it also has to figure out how to meet all the regulations—and do it profitably. Since the regulations come from an outside agency with authority, the priority has to be the *what* and *how* they meet regulatory scrutiny—before profitability is considered. Failure to meet regulations regardless of profitability runs the risk of sanctions and penalties from the authoritative body. If they can't figure out how to do it profitably, they will be out of business. For privately held organizations, regulation becomes the compelling driver to figure out how to deliver the product or service profitably—while meeting all regulations.

In contrast, unregulated organizations have the pressure of profitability—but not so much the pressure of regulation.[9] They have a fundamental difference in the way they can operate when compared to regulated organizations. Unregulated organizations have to decide if there is an advantage to delivering their product and service in a highly reliable fashion or if it is better not to worry about that and just focus on short-term profitability. This

---

[9]   Although all industry is regulated to some degree, I am referring to industries, such as pharmaceutical, aviation, and nuclear, that are highly regulated and subject to routine and random auditing and self-reporting to an outside government agency.

heavily weighted focus on short-term profitability causes many organizations to fail to become LeadeReliable. They create a decision point around short-term profits versus long-term steady growth. They desire long-term steady growth, but sometimes the lust for short-term profits clouds their view. When a choice of profits or long-term steady growth must be made, short-term profits often wins out. Short-term profits cover the losses created by a lack of reliability. The lack of proactive mitigation of the impact of unplanned events and acceptance of them causes them to have significant and repeated failures, which ultimately create wasted resources and lost profits. As a result, they use short-term profits to cover their losses.

Acceptance that unplanned events are normal is flawed thinking. Organizations that treat anything unplanned as abnormal become more proactive and more profitable. They address the abnormal unplanned event before it is disruptive and costly. They have more profits and resources to use and can make different decisions around short-term profits and long-term growth.

What would it take for an unregulated organization to create the same compelling reason to perform at a level of high reliability without significant external regulation? What becomes the compelling reason not to be simply satisfied with living in a reactive culture and press on toward LeadeReliability? What would motivate the organization to become self-regulated and reap the constant and consistent delivery of product or service and maximize profit and margins?

First, let's explore why regulations occur in the first place.

Regulatory bodies are put in place typically to ensure safety of the operation and the products or services delivered. The airline industry is regulated, but it is similar to many other unregulated organizations that have to maintain profitability to survive. When speaking of the airline industry, it is safe to assume that the regulatory agency (primarily the Federal Aviation Agency) is more worried about the company complying with regulations than it is with the organization's profitability. However, the reverse is true for the company. The company has to worry about profitability and fully comply with all regulations. How do they make it work?

Airlines have discovered that it is much more profitable to deliver their products and services reliably and compliantly than to have regulating agencies dictate their actions. People always laugh when I talk about reliability and airlines; after all, most of us have experienced being stranded in an airport because a plane was delayed or cancelled. As a result, we stand in line to complain about how unreliable the airline is. However, upon closer consideration, when you look at airlines, their first level of reliability—their primary constant and consistent commitment—must be the absolute assurance that a plane will take off and land safely while meeting all regulations. In the broad scheme of reliability, the choice not to fly because of an unsafe condition or a violation of regulation is the only reliable decision they can make. With the decision comes an impact on profitability. The more reliable and compliant an airline can be, the higher the chance of profitability.

A case in point is Delta Air Lines. It starts at the top at Delta. CEO Richard Anderson constantly and consistently focuses on reliability. Because of that focus, everything that Delta does is focused on doing it reliably, and every person in the organization knows that they are part of the solution.[10, 11] His focus on reliability has turned the profitability of the corporation around while still meeting regulatory compliance. Delta made $1.6 billion in profit for 2012.[12] This is a $400 million increase from 2011, and things continue to improve even though the economy is soft. A company that was in bankruptcy six years ago is now the Fortune 500's

---

[10] History of Delta, www.delta.com.
[11] Yahoo AP report, December 14, 2011.
[12] *The Atlanta Journal Constitution*, AJC.com, December 12, 2012.

eighty-third ranked company,[13] and an organizational focus on reliability deserves some of the credit.[14]

Reliability has a place in driving profitability and meeting regulations. What would a focus on reliability deliver to an unregulated company—and why do unregulated companies have such a problem becoming highly reliable?

Unplanned events are totally disruptive to the ability to be reliable and the ability to be profitable. Every unplanned event detracts from both. When an unplanned event occurs, the organization spends money and resources to remedy the situation. During that period of remediation, none of that resource expenditure goes toward generating profit. I refer to this as Cash Outflow without Sales (COWS); in a sense, every organization does not want that herd to get very big. They would like to get completely out of the cattle business. Every dollar spent on remediation of an unplanned event is a dollar not spent to create revenue. The sooner an unplanned event can be detected and addressed, the less that has to be spent dealing with it.

If you look at Delta pre-2007, I would guess that—although they knew they needed to make a profit—their emphasis must have been more on regulatory compliance. Their bankruptcy proved they couldn't make a profit. Today they remain compliant with regulations and profitable—a powerful difference.

Understanding what needs to be done and doing it while minimizing unplanned events creates the lowest long-term cost platform for doing anything. When you minimize the impact of unplanned events, fewer resources are spent on the need to do things again to get them right; this is clearly the most efficient way of doing anything. If reliability is perceived as a cost rather than an advantage, this approach might be missed. The fallacies discussed

---

[13] Money.cnn.com\magazine\fortune 500.
[14] Personal benchmarking study conducted in 2011 during a personal visit to Delta Airlines corporate headquarters in Atlanta.

in the previous chapter are simply not true. Like Delta, if the entire organization focuses on reliability and makes it the responsibility of each and every person, reliability and profitability can coexist and thrive. They feed off of each other to the advantage of all.

Some organizations try to inject reliability into the process after the fact. Their mind-set is that you only need a portion of the organization worried about constantly and consistently delivering on commitments. We were able to see in the last chapter how that approach to reliability could be very costly. If the creation of reliability is always thought of as "someone else's job" and not the job of each member of the organization, then constantly and consistently meeting commitments is hard. This additional staffing may cause the final product and service to be delivered reliably—but with much more expense and effort than is needed. Organizations must create compelling reasons for every individual to take the minimization of the impact of unplanned events as a personal responsibility and not as the job of someone else.

To experience the same levels of improved reliability and profitability experienced by some regulated organizations, unregulated companies must develop the culture and discipline to become highly reliable—and they must do it without an external force driving them in that direction. This lack of external force, coupled with the misconception that reliability is costly, is what keeps most corporations from achieving LeadeReliability throughout the organization, and it is a leading reason why organizations stop trying.

Although previously discussed, it is worth reiterating because of the significant mind-set impact after-the-fact checking has on the culture. Putting in a quality checking organization could be looked at as being very proactive because the activity happens before the customer. Organizations that do this realize that bad product can't get to the customer, so they put in the extra layer of "proactive" protection to try to ensure that it doesn't. As a result, every individual in the organization is not expected to make reliable, long-term decisions for themselves because it is not really their job. It is accepted practice that whatever they fail to discover will be caught by someone else whose job it is to do that. Depending on the individuals involved, they may leave the task of reliability to those whose job it is. This organization, although appearing proactive, actually has become reactive because most reliability is built in after the fact.

What about the cultural ramifications of this post-inspection approach rather than creating LeadeReliability? LeadeReliability requires constancy and consistency of message and action by the organization to meet the commitments. Organizations that put in another layer of "inspectors" to ensure quality, reliability, or productivity have done two things that detract from the benefits of LeadeReliability. They have increased the cost of achieving the desired state, and they have essentially told those who are not "inspectors" that looking for abnormal is not their job. Both of these have a negative impact on reliability. In organizations that are highly reliable, every person in the organization takes on the responsibility of "inspectors," and everyone has the desire to do something to minimize unplanned events. Each member of the organization has to say "I need to do something about reliability," and not "Someone needs to do something about reliability."

The external pressure on most unregulated companies is profitability—not compliance with regulations (which drives reliability). This pressure may create a short-term focus that could actually cause decisions that damage long-term reliability. They also could have a negative impact on developing a reliability culture and long-term financial success.

With an external pressure of profitability (investors, analysts, shareholders, etc.) decisions are often made that put investments in reliability on hold to take on more immediate profits. Resources spent on becoming more reliable are always an investment and never a cost. The question is whether the organization can afford to invest in reliability or whether they are more interested in taking the profits and walking away from the investment. This is always a decision for an unregulated organization. Meeting regulations, which we know drive reliability of product delivery and quality, are not optional; without those regulations, the investment in reliability that delivers the same effect can be put off.

With the pressing dilemma of outside pressure for profits, how can a LeadeReliability mind-set become embraced? Minimizing the impact of unplanned events has to be the focus all the time— not just when the economy is good or during a certain project. It must become a way of life for all individuals in the organization and the focus of the way they think. They should approach each situation and determine the most reliable way to deliver the product or service. How can they do what they do and minimize the chances that resources will be wasted before the customer is satisfied?

LeadeReliability requires a focus on being reliable. That sounds like a simple statement, but it's not simple for the unregulated organization that focuses on short-term profits and not on reliability. When you read this statement, it sounds almost preposterous that reliability and profitability are mutually exclusive. Preposterous or not, that is exactly what some people think and is the source of fallacies already discussed. Once LeadeReliability is established, the notion that reliability enhances profits becomes an absolute, but during the transition, the temptation is always to focus exclusively on immediate profits, even if it jeopardizes long-term ones.

Here is where tough decisions to create LeadeReliability must be made. If you are focused on long-term reliability, you may be required to make decisions that make sense in the long run, but analysts and Wall Street might not agree with you because those decisions may impact immediate profits. The choice may be short-term profits or long-term reliability and long-term profitability—a decision that is sometimes tough to make. It is a decision that takes courage and commitment, but we can look to regulated organizations for proof of success of the later choice.

Richard Anderson reported that Delta would be solidly profitable in 2012—even though fuel prices would remain higher than historic averages and the economy still would be soft. He reiterated that the company would do all this and still cut 2012 flying time by 2-3 percent.[15, 16] His predictions held true. His focus on reliability caused the value of Delta stock (DAL) to triple in eighteen months.[17] The improvement didn't happen immediately, but because reliability is a long-term value approach, when it begins to create value, it does it dramatically. Through a focus on reliability, Delta has proven that you can become more profitable—even if you cut the amount of flying time and have increased operation costs. This story proves that LeadeReliability will lead to customer loyalty, employee engagement, and increased profits regardless of the economic climate.

Therefore, one mind-set that is required to become LeadeReliable is the concept of defining what self-regulation means to your organization—and then having the courage to apply it and stick to it.

CREATE A REASON TO CARE.

The other LeadeReliability mind-set necessary to be successful is creating a reason to care about what is happening inside the organization. Many individuals who work inside an organization are mentally engaged and give their efforts, but when asked, they would tell you that they don't really care about what the organizations is doing. It is a job, a task, or something they do, but they really don't care. To create LeadeReliability, all people, in their own mind, must develop a reason to care. With this reason, they develop the discipline that they hold themselves

---

[15]   Yahoo AP report, December 14, 2011.

[16]   *The Atlanta Journal Constitution*, AJC.com, December 12, 2012.

[17]   Based on DAL stock price, May 15, 2013.

personally accountable for their own actions and the outcome of their actions toward the minimization of the impact of unplanned events. Without this unanimous personal accountability in an organization, the concept of LeadeReliability will always struggle to exist and never can reach its fullest potential.

Every organization has a culture and is highly dependent on what matters to the leaders and the majority in the culture. These are usually the same because the leaders typically mold the majority point of view. The organization's mind-set depends very much on what the organization thinks is important and what it holistically thinks about concepts and situations. Any service, manufacturing, volunteer, nonprofit, or even family organization will establish a culture that becomes its personality. This personality creates a strong bias for what the organization believes is important. These become the critical things that drive the organization's direction and intent. It will become what the organization cares and talks about. If reliability is not one of these priorities, then creating LeadeReliability will never happen.

Most organizations want to run at the lowest cost and at the highest revenues possible to have the largest margins. That being said, through LeadeReliability and the minimization of the impact of unplanned events, we have begun to establish that the lowest-cost way to run any organization is to never have to repeat activities. In essence, constantly and consistently meeting the commitments that have been laid out and the resources used will deliver the optimum profit.

Likewise, the way to create the highest revenues is to have a product or service that is deeply desired by your customers or the recipients of your services—and those customers and recipients are constantly and consistently willing to accept the delivery of your product or service at an agreed-upon frequency and price. There is a denominator and numerator to the margin equation. Profit is the total revenue less the total cost of creating that revenue, and the margin is that profit divided by the cost.

Profit equals revenue minus total cost of creating revenue.
Percent margin equals profit divide by cost.

Therefore, to impact margin, you can increase the profit by increasing revenue and reducing cost or you can increase profit to a lesser extent by only doing one of these. Reducing cost can typically be done much quicker than increasing revenue. Reducing cost usually requires stopping doing something rather than doing more of something. Increasing revenue is usually the opposite. It requires doing more rather than doing less of something.

Based on B. F. Skinner's work in the area of behavioral science, most people and organizations prefer consequences that are personal, immediate, and certain rather than those that are personal, future, and uncertain. Elimination of cost is the former, and creation of new revenue is the latter. Therefore, most organizations lean first toward cost reduction rather than revenue creation when they want to impact margin quickly. Those who have not thought a lot about changing the reliability culture will always lean toward cutting cost as the first course of action. The extrapolation is that to operate at the lowest cost, you must create a cost-cutting culture and not a reliability one. This could be the case in certain economic situations where affordability or survival is the immediate question. However, for the longer, more sustained culture development and the long-term viability of an organization, I believe this is the wrong approach. Without focusing on developing a reliability culture, the significance of unplanned events, the significant loss of resources, and the increased cost of operation are never addressed. Also because of the lack of ability to constantly and consistently meet commitments, the loss of revenue through unsatisfied customers is a very real probability.

Organizations that are willing to move the culture toward LeadeReliability discover that the creation of reliability through cultural change—by minimizing the impact of unplanned events and meeting customer commitments—is a much more powerful approach. LeadeReliability drives the minimization of cost—technically and culturally. Without culture change, even if there is a technical focus on reliability, unplanned events continue to occur. Since LeadeReliability creates customer loyalty and employee engagement, it has the ability to increase profits and reduce costs. Reliability efforts that do not address cultural change only impact costs.

Although not directly intuitive, the creation of LeadeReliability and the driving behavior toward individual reliability is significantly more impactful than any money spent on reliability issues. If you attempt to spend significant sums of money to create reliability and don't create a culture of behaviors that minimizes the impact of unplanned events, the only certainty is that you will continue to spend at that level because the minimization of the impact of unplanned events will never be addressed. Conversely, if the focus is to create LeadeReliability, the resources that were wasted on unplanned events can now be refocused on the efforts the organization strives to achieve. Spending is optimized, and resources are put against the most impactful activities that create even further reliability and resulting profits. The culmination of this effort will be an organization that has the optimum resource distribution, the lowest costs, and the highest margin based on the revenue stream.

How does LeadeReliability begin?

To begin the journey, it takes one person with enough passionate desire to constantly and consistently deliver on every commitment. That person must believe and understand that the impact of all unplanned events can be minimized. That person has to be someone brave enough to share his or her thoughts and be passionate enough to deal with any resistance. They must have enough courage to keep pushing until another person develops a reason to care.

ACADEMIC TO PASSIONATE

If that notion is true, then the only way to get an entire culture to change is to move the understanding of every person from an academic one about why the impact of unplanned events should be minimized to a passionate desire to minimize them. Academically, everyone will agree that there should be fewer unplanned events, but do they really care? Only when they develop their own reason to minimize the impact of unplanned events and a passionate desire to meet commitments will they be able to influence another.

The journey toward LeadeReliability does not have to start with the organizational leaders. However, their influence is essential to total success. The majority typically understands and follows what these leaders care about. In order for the journey to move forward at an efficient pace, the organizational leaders must develop their own reasons to care about minimizing the impact of unplanned events and meeting commitments. Once they do, they can further influence others in the organization to develop reasons for caring. If they don't, the journey will be much more difficult because these leaders will focus on something other than meeting commitments and minimizing the impact of unplanned events. To be as successful as possible, every individual in the organization has to figure out why they care. If one person doesn't develop the passion, they may notice the early stages of the unplanned event and take no action. The unplanned event's impact will not be minimized at best—and end up in disaster at worst. Each person has to develop a mind-set that shows they care.

Sam McNair's work on the correlation between spending money on maintenance resources versus working on the culture shows the significant impact that culture change has on reliability.[18] He defines five types of cultures that he has seen exist in organizations—from "out of control," which I call chaos to "excellence," which is LeadeReliability.

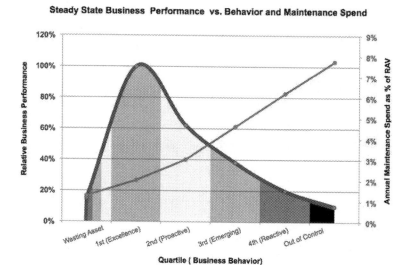

Steady State Business Performance vs. Behavior and Maintenance Spend

Through his extensive research and benchmarking, Sam shows that only through "excellence" can the highest relative business performance be achieved (the dark thick gray line represents the level which the organization meets a customer's needs) at the lowest cost (thin gray line) for that business performance. Any movement of the culture back toward "out of control" will

---

[18]   The chart below was extracted from a white paper by Sam McNair of Life Cycle Engineering. It assumes that your facility is at a steady state and basically maintainable level (neither improving nor deteriorating and performance is at least acceptable). The data is a result of extensive benchmarking. Source: White paper "Budgeting for Maintenance: A Behavior-Based Approach by Sam McNair" of Life Cycle Engineering. This data can be applied to any stable plant. The estimates vary slightly because of plant age and a small amount by industry type and location. It's driven almost entirely by organizational behaviors or competencies.

create less business performance and require more resources. Any cultural movement toward wasting, although requiring fewer resources, causes rapid business performance deterioration and has the same impact as "out of control."

This study validates the notion that creating a culture of LeadeReliability is the most cost-effective way to run an organization.

CHAPTER 5

THE HEART OF RELIABILITY

I am not bound to succeed, but I am bound
to live up to what light I have.
—Abraham Lincoln

W e have already established the need for self-regulation and a reason to care that allows us to change how we think about reliability. We transform from an academic agreement to a passionate belief. It requires one person to be so passionate about that belief that he or she is willing to start the cultural change. Let's look deeper into how that happens.

A definition of psychology is the mental characteristics of a person or a group. LeadeReliability requires the psychology concerning leadership and reliability to change. With a case for considering LeadeReliability firmly established, we see why a person or group might consider starting the journey. Most cultural change starts with a person. Martin Luther King Jr., Nelson Mandela, and Abraham Lincoln all led cultural change because they disagreed with all or part of the culture they were living in. They decided individually that something needed to be changed. Through their passion, influence, and stamina, they initiated change in the culture and were persistent, brave, and patient enough to move it toward completion. Although two of the three's lives were cut short by opposition, their legacies remain strong.

Cultural change and the journey toward LeadeReliability start with the individual. That person has to be so committed to the change and so committed to driving it that he or she will not stop until they have inspired the change in others. This person's passionate belief in himself or herself drives him or her even though many others will have little or no interest in these ideas at the onset. Some may be completely opposed to what the person sees so clearly and thinks must be created.

If it all starts with the individual, what causes that individual's heart to stir? The personal change starts a significant journey. It may occur over time or from a Damascus Road experience, but the personal transition moves the concept, idea, or desire for change from an academic notion in the brain to a passionate obsession in the heart. The person moves the concept they are dealing with from something they have thought about or know about, to something they care deeply about. That passion compels them to lead the change.

When Rosa Parks refused to move her seat on that bus in Montgomery, Alabama, in 1955, and was arrested for civil disobedience, much of the community thought the treatment of this woman and her subsequent arrest were morally and ethically wrong. However, no one did anything about it until a group of leaders, led by E. D. Nixon and Ralph Abernathy, asked Martin Luther King Jr. to lead the Montgomery Bus Boycott. Through his leadership and that small beginning, the ember of civil discontent that had smoldered for years turned into a flame called the American civil rights movement. For the next twelve years, this young clergyman used his personal passion to change and influence history.

Whatever the idea, whatever the concept, each person must have a reason to care about something to engage in it. It is a matter of the heart and not one of the head. What a person is passionate about is what they care about—and what they care about is what they are passionate about. It is a continuous dynamic that feeds itself. The process of LeadeReliability starts with personal reliability. How do you get people to care about a family, group, team, organization, or corporation? How do you capture their hearts?

In John Maxwell's *The 21 Irrefutable Laws of Leadership*, he talks about the law of connection. He says, "Leaders touch a heart before they ask for a hand." He talks about the importance of "heart capture." Why is capturing the heart so important? It gives a person a reason to care.

When I was in high school, I spent two years in Spanish class. I remember how to say *hola* and can count to ten. Why don't I know Spanish—and why didn't I learn it enough to be able to speak it now? I took Spanish classes for a few reasons, and none of them were based in my heart. My reason to take Spanish was purely academic. As a result, my effort to learn the language failed. Beyond academics and getting a passing grade, I really didn't care if I learned Spanish. I took Spanish because there was a second language requirement at my high school and at the university I planned on attending. It had nothing to do with a desire to learn how to speak Spanish. The concept of academic understanding is that you agree with the concept or the subject; in passionate understanding, you care about the concept or the subject.

While I was struggling with Spanish and learning just enough to pass the next test, I was thoroughly enjoying American history. Why? It was easy because my teacher was passionate about history. He loved history and made each class an adventure. He taught passionately and captured my heart. History became something I cared about. It was not that Spanish wasn't an interesting topic— and it wasn't that my Spanish teacher didn't have a passion for the subject—but I could not relate to Spanish on the same level that I could relate to history. My heart was primed for a reason to care about American history. The way it was taught put my heart over the edge and gave me that reason. I still have the same passion for history because I know that we learn from our history or are destined to repeat it. I have experienced both a number of times.

Capturing the heart of someone takes the availability of the heart and a stimulus—internal or external—that triggers the move from the head to the heart. American history was something I cared about because I was a young man growing up in America and had played military and Old West games during my childhood. Then when I took American history, I had someone who could teach and deliver the topic in such a way that I developed the same passion for history as he had. That passion made me care about American history, and today it translates to all history. Passion for something causes it to grow.

Let's explore these two things—availability of the heart and the internal or external stimulus—when it comes to the development of LeadeReliability. Why should an individual care about becoming part of a group that bases its heart, mental energy, and behaviors on LeadeReliability? He or she must develop a reason to care.

Let's first look at what LeadeReliability does for an individual. We can look at the negative to determine what a lack of reliability does to an individual. One thing that lack of reliability robs from a person is time. We typically have two types of days—ones that go smoothly and ones that don't. The ones that do not are typically disrupted by an unplanned event. Something has gone wrong. You were planning to accomplish something, go someplace, or participate in some activity, but something external completely disrupted your plans. As a result, you didn't accomplish what you had planned on doing. The result of that disruption must be dealt with. If it was something that must be accomplished, you still have to do it. If it was something you were planning on doing because it would deliver you pleasure or meet a need, you just missed it. It could have been a single event that has passed. As you know, this can happen in work and leisure. When it does, it potentially creates stress because you know you still have to get it done or creates disappointment because you know you missed it. Neither of these are satisfying feelings. If too many of these instances occur, things tend to build up and can impact your health and well-being.

An unplanned event can create short-term disruption or long-term issues. Unplanned events are the result of unreliability in the system. Something happened that did not constantly or consistently deliver what was intended. As a result, your day was disrupted. The sad state that develops is that some of us get to the point where abnormal disruptions like this are perceived as normal and a way of life. We allow them to continue to roll over us without much thought, but it could be different. For every individual who is impacted by this type of occurrence, there is a ripple effect. Since this person may not be able to deliver constantly and consistently on their commitments, they can create an unplanned event for someone else. Depending on the situation, the impact of the first unplanned event could become exponential.

The second thing that personal unreliability takes away is trust. We become untrustworthy because of our actions or someone else becomes untrustworthy to us. Rarely is this intentional, but the abnormal becomes normal.

Let's discuss a simple example where this is the case. Let's say you have a good friend who is always late—and that lateness ranges from ten to thirty minutes. When you are planning on meeting with this person, what do you do? Once you establish a time to meet, do you trust that they will be there? Do you play games with the meeting time so your time is not wasted? You might believe they will not be on time, but you treat the abnormal as normal. Where does the inability to be trusted end? Is it only about being on time—or does it spread to other things? When you are planning something together and are waiting on this person, what are you thinking about? Are you getting to do what you planned? Your attitude toward this person's reliability will be swayed, and it will impact how you think about them in regard to other things. If this person said they needed to meet you someplace at a certain time, would you trust that they would be there? You can see how this simple issue can grow into a lack of trust. Personal reliability is the key to trust; the more you can depend on someone constantly and consistently meeting their commitments, the more you will trust them.

Extrapolate this to a group or organization to see how the group or organization develops the same reputation. That larger entity is known by some level of reliability that is an extrapolation of the individuals who make up the group. The interesting thing is that it does not take the entire organization to act a certain way. The behavior of individuals in the group translates to what is thought of the organization. This is the main reason why every individual in the organization has to create personal reliability. If someone who is not reliable is the view of the organization in someone's eyes, there is a chance the entire organization is painted with that same view. The organization is known by circumstances or events that are brought about by individuals who make or don't make decisions that impact how an event transpires. We continue to see the importance of every individual in the organization, participating actively in developing personal reliability, because his or her action or inaction creates someone's opinion of the entire organization.

Reliability can be a foundation for everything—individually and organization-wise. If you constantly and consistently meet the commitments you have made, you will create the foundation to create LeadeReliability. With reliability, there is a good chance that each day will not be disrupted and individuals can plan on doing what they set out to do. They will be able to develop a sense of trust with others in the group, organization, or corporation that will transcend internally and have an external impact. It will become how individuals and the organization are perceived by others.

That is reliability. In simple terms, it is an individual or group who constantly and consistently delivers on what they say they are going to do. It is a great way to establish a sound and strong foundation for being reliable.

Unfortunately, not many people respond emotionally to what people do, but they do respond to why they do it. When it comes to LeadeReliability, why should someone care?

In a great conversation that is displayed on www.ted.com, which is a website subtitled "ideas worth sharing," Simon Sinek[19] talks about the significance of why individuals and organizations do things versus what and how. He explores why some people and companies have an advantage in achieving things when others can't. His discovery profoundly changed his own world view. He has discovered that great leaders communicate in a way that is very different from others who are not. He calls it the "golden circle." *What* on the outside—*how* and *why* as you work toward the middle.

Most people tell you what they do, how they do it, and finally why they do it. Sinek believes *why* is the most important thing. He discovered that all great inspirational leaders think from the inside of the "golden circle" out. They don't start with what and work to why. They start with why and work to what. It is why that inspires others. When it comes to reliability, you have to create passion through why. Why should you and others become reliable? You must discover why for yourself and then for your organization. Sinek proposes that we first communicate with the part of the brain that spurs feeling and drives behavior—and then we allow the what part of the brain to justify that behavior. When it comes to individual reliability, what is your *why*? Why will your

---

[19] Simon Sinek, *Start with Why: How Great Leaders Inspire Everyone to Take Action* (Penguin Books, 2009). Much of this discussion is validated by Simon Sinek's work.

heart be captured? When it comes to reliability or anything else, people respond much more to why than what.

Sinek refers to Malcolm Gladwell's work in *The Tipping Point: How Little Things Can Make a Big Difference* and points out different segments of people in every population—innovators, early adopters, early majority, late majority, and laggards—and how they have different reasons for acting the ways they do.

Early adopters and innovators make their decisions based on why, and the early majority wait and follow what the early adopters do. Sinek says that the innovators typically make up 2.5 percent of the population, and the early adopters make up roughly 13.5 percent. If you can inspire these two groups with the why, the early majority will be watching and follow what the innovators and early adopters do. If the desire is to move an organization toward LeadeReliability, great gains can be made by capturing a small percentage of the key influencers in an organization. Gladwell, in his book, refers to this as the law of diffusion of innovation. In order for an idea to gain momentum, the tipping point must be achieved. This occurs when you reach 15-18 percent of the population (innovators, early adopters, and the beginning of the early majority). The system tips, and the rest of the early majority will follow because they are anxious to try new things but won't until someone else does. To create LeadeReliability, figuring out how to capture the hearts of the innovators and early adopters is critical. What are some of the reasons why they should care?

Each individual will decide. There are as many reasons to care about what LeadeReliability can do for you as there are people who care. The reason why is a personal decision, and it evolves out of values, desires, and needs. One person may be anxious to get some balance in their life and they see the benefits of LeadeReliability. Another may really want the business they work in to succeed and realize that LeadeReliability is the right path. Reasons to care span from completely personal to completely professional. Something in the concept of getting to do what you planned on doing could sway some. For others, the notion of moving out of chaos could be the key. Peeling the onion of issue resolution to create benefit for individuals and organizations will cause others to want to learn more and attempt to minimize the impact of unplanned events. Every person who takes a step toward LeadeReliability could influence others to follow.

Heart captured. It may be a word, an example, or an observation, but something captures the heart. Something moves the person from academic interest to passionate involvement. From "someone needs to do something" about reliability to "I will do something" about reliability is the transition that occurs once the heart is captured. A measure of how much you care is how much time you spend talking about it. We tend to spend time talking about the things we care about the most. How much time do you spend talking about, thinking about, and spending time with your best friend compared to an acquaintance that you only see once in a while? Your best friend has captured your heart. LeadeReliability could become a very good friend.

Journey from the head to the heart. How this journey occurs is different for every person. It is almost impossible to understand and know what will cause you to make this twelve-inch journey from the head to the heart, but you will know it when it happens. How much you care about something will become much more profound. Think about all the things you really care about and think about the things you just know about. This is one way to measure whether you really care about LeadeReliability.

LeadeReliability becomes a way of life. LeadeReliability becomes how you do everything, and you instinctively take actions that minimize the impact of unplanned events. You don't really have to think about doing it—you just do it. You transition your belief about LeadeReliability from something you have to do to how you do everything. Walking down the steps, working, driving, sharing what you know with others, and preparing for your day are all done as reliably as possible. If it is compelling, it will capture the hearts of the innovators and early adopters—but what comes next?

LeadeReliability becomes contagious. Not everyone is an innovator or an early adopter, and some may even be in the late majority, but whenever someone begins to care about minimizing the impact of unplanned events, he or she will be amazed at how contagious the behavior becomes. There is quick realization that a planned, less stressed, less interrupted life is more productive when there is focus on LeadeReliability. Those who don't experience it will see it in others who do. Once the calmness of LeadeReliability is discovered—and it is how those involved do everything—others will notice. Hearts will be captured by some who are not even aware of it.

Start hearing the words. One of the early indicators that the movement is taking hold is that you start to hear much more conversation about LeadeReliability. Words and phrases like minimization of unplanned events, root-cause investigation, reduction of cost due to increased reliability, proactively looking at leading indicators, resilience,[20] preoccupation with failure, deference to expertise, sensitivity to operations, reluctance to simplify, and others be discussed. These words create awareness and raise curiosity from others; in many cases, a new language centered

---

[20] The behaviors listed—resilience, preoccupied with failure, deference to expertise, sensitivity to operations, and reluctance to simplify—are the behaviors identified by Weick and Sutcliffe in *Managing the Unexpected*, Karl E. Weick and Kathleen M. Sutcliffe, John Wiley & Sons, 2007

on LeadeReliability develops. Individuals translate these concepts for themselves—personally and professionally—and apply them to their everyday lives.

The tipping point is reached. As described above, the law of diffusion of innovation says that movements and cultures take hold once 15-18 percent of the population begins to care. As this begins to occur, the movement or culture change has a great chance of succeeding. Even if a person is not one of the innovators or early adopters, his or her zeal and passion for LeadeReliability may be the thing that captures another's heart. When that person begins to change their words and actions, it may capture someone else's heart.

The majority takes action. As the early majority begins to care about LeadeReliability because their heart is captured, there comes a point when the majority of the organization begins to take action in a way that begins to minimize unplanned events. This causes the movement of the organization toward LeadeReliability to accelerate. When the majority reaches its tipping point, the advantages become obvious and even desired. More members of the organization are working to minimize the impact of unplanned events than aren't.

Laggards convert or leave. After the late majority has made the move to LeadeReliability, there is a small percentage of the organization that could be described as laggards. This small group is comfortable with the way things are and are very comfortable in agreeing with the minimization of the impact of unplanned events, but they are quick to say "Someone should do something about it." These folks are the last people who must be converted to LeadeReliability—or they must leave so the organization to be completely converted to LeadeReliability. By their very nature, unplanned events start at some level of disruption and get worse with time. If an individual sees the beginning of an unplanned event and says "Someone needs to do something," it will take another person to discover the unplanned event before its impact can be minimized. Since these situations are dynamic, the impact will be worse than if it had been addressed initially. Changing the laggard's behaviors is essential. The disruption caused by nonresponse and lack of accountability will cause peer pressure. Since the large majority of members of the organization say, "I need to do something," lack of accountability will not be tolerated. The remaining individuals must make a choice. They must figure out how they can turn their understanding from academic to passionate and develop reasons to care or they must leave. Staying is the best choice for everyone because of the time invested and the knowledge and experience that can be put to use, but if the reason to care can't be created, then removing them from the organization is the only option. LeadeReliability minimizes the impact of all unplanned events—and weak links can't exist.

What about new employees? When new employees come into a culture where everyone says, "I need to do something about minimizing unplanned events" and actually do it, they come into a culture where people have time to think and time to innovate. They come into a culture of leadership at all levels. What will they do? They quickly realize they must do the same things to be successful—and that is what they do.

Daily choices. Each day will be one of disruption, turmoil, and reacting to unplanned events or a day that you get to do what you planned on doing and you accomplish the things you think are important. The difference is how work gets done. A focus on LeadeReliability will deliver more days where planned work gets done, and there will be fewer days of disruption. For an organization, group, or individual, LeadeReliability is a preferred state that is only accomplished through individual reliability for the person or organizational reliability for the group. Each person must develop a reason to care and must develop personal accountability, which can be interjected into the organization.

CHAPTER 6

ESSENTIALS FOR EXECUTING THE CULTURE

The method of the enterprising is to plan with
audacity and execute with vigor.
—Christian Nestell Bovee

U p until this point, we have spent a lot of time talking
about what LeadeReliability looks like, why it is important,
and what benefits will be derived from the journey. We have
mentioned the need to create a culture—and that it can't be an
initiative or a program. We have said it is a journey that requires
passion, commitment, and time. How does it happen? How is the
culture created? What events have to take place?

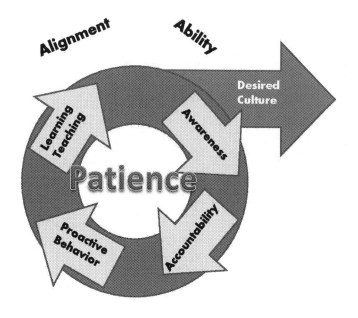

ALIGNMENT AND ABILITY

This culture journey starts with alignment and ability. The alignment comes from an innovator who convinces one other person and *then* a small group or team to think about and consider beginning the journey toward LeadeReliability. The idea of the minimization of the impact of unplanned events by constantly and consistently keeping commitments becomes important to at least one individual. The one person who has the vision or idea has to believe so strongly in that vision that they are willing to share it with another. They then focus on another and develop a willingness to attempt to inspire someone else with their vision. If the person is able to inspire a few more people, the mission for that group becomes to constantly and consistently meet commitments and minimize the impact of unplanned events. That is all it takes to get started, and this focus must be on the journey. As mentioned previously, distractions and interference will crop up along the way, but LeadeReliability must be the basis of the journey and the ultimate goal.

If there is deviation from this goal, the culture will end up someplace else. Most likely, there will be a reversion to where the culture was or the culture will be created based on one of the distractions or points of interference. It will not be LeadeReliability; it will revert or evolve into something else. A leader creates the direction, and as others become leaders on the journey, they ensure that they keep the organization pointed in that direction.

It sounds simple, but it isn't if distractions prevail. Once the alignment is established, the evaluation of ability begins. Every organization and person in the organization from the beginning has some ability to constantly and consistently keep their commitments and the ability to minimize the impact of unplanned events—even if they have never thought about it. It is done all the time without much thought. Millions of times each day, individuals and organizations keep their commitments and minimize the impact of unplanned events. They don't do it all the time because they haven't trained themselves to think about it. They still believe that it is normal for unplanned events to happen.

Individuals and organizations are not as reliable as they could be. Too much is left on the table. Most organizations spend 10 percent of their revenue on unplanned events and waste forty days dealing with the fallout from them. The opportunity for improvement is huge if we become more reliable. Each time we minimize the impact of an unplanned event, we take that portion of the significant opportunity and direct the resources toward a planned activity, which creates value. Since without thinking about it there is some ability to minimize the impact of unplanned events, that will be the starting point. As the focus of more and more of the organization becomes that minimization of the impact of unplanned events, the negative impact of them will become less. As the culture develops you will be able to compare back to the starting point to determine how much success you are achieving. I will go more into how to do this later in the book.

Awareness

Once you have alignment, you have created a level of awareness. However, awareness is a fleeting condition; people on a continuous basis become more or less aware. What drives awareness is the constant reminder of what it is you are concerned about, dealing with, or what is important to you. What decreases awareness is no longer thinking, talking, or caring about that issue. Awareness creates knowledge.

Awareness is defined as knowing something; having knowledge of something from having observed or been told about it; noticing or realizing something; knowing that something exists because you notice it or realize that it is happening

Knowledgeable is defined as well informed about what is going on in the world or about the latest developments in a sphere of activity

The more we can raise awareness about a particular action, the more likely it is that a person might care about that subject—or at least have the wherewithal to decide whether he or she does. If awareness is not raised or developed, the chances of the person even considering the issue—let alone caring about it—is slim.

We know about, talk about, and think about the things we are aware of. Let's consider unplanned events. If we are predisposed to believe that they are a normal occurrence of life and there is not much you can do about them, you won't spend much time thinking about them. You will be convinced that they are normal occurrences. However, if you become aware of LeadeReliability and think that unplanned events are abnormal and can be minimized through action, you will immediately do something about them.

How can awareness be raised on any subject? Here is a simple, effective example of how awareness can be raised about any subject. Once you see this example, you will see the essential key to raising awareness.

My birthday is December 1. Through my intelligence sources (just kidding), I know not one of you cares because you have never sent me a card or a present. If you never hear about this again, but I walk up behind you, tap you on the shoulder, and ask you when my birthday is, there is a very good chance you will ask, "Who is this strange person?" I would wager a lot of money that you would not know. You heard about my birthday once—and that was it. You were made aware, but that awareness was not reinforced.

However, I can change that. I can almost guarantee that you will remember my birthday from now on. Again through my intelligence sources, I have obtained your work and your personal e-mail addresses. Beginning today, I will send my picture and the date of my birthday to both and occasionally to your home. Just to raise the awareness more, my picture will be in various types of dress—leisure, business, exercise, or vacation. Even if you delete the messages, the subject line will say my name and my birthday. To prevent you from blocking these e-mails, I will change my e-mail address periodically. A very intense state of awareness on this subject will be established. No matter where in the world you are, if I tap you on the shoulder (possibly completely out of context), when I ask you my birthday, you will say, "I hate you . . . December 1."

I have sufficiently raised your awareness to the point that you naturally respond to that question. The way I did it was by reminding you or talking about it all the time. This is the key to creating awareness. If you want to raise awareness about something, you have to talk about it all the time. It has to become part of you, and you have to be constantly aware of it. If we want to drive awareness about minimizing the impact of unplanned events, you have to talk about it all the time. The more you talk about it, the more people will think about it because we talk about the things we care about—and the things we care about are the things we take interest in and try to positively impact.

I have one more thing to share that will reinforce how talking about something all the time when it comes to what you care about is important. It has to deal with learning a language.

At one point in my career, I was responsible for a number of manufacturing facilities in Germany. One of the things that bothered me—and continues to bother me—is not being able to speak another language. The people I was working with were often able to speak mine. I realize that English is the business language of the world, but it has always bothered me. I also realize that I would not be able to learn every language for every country, but since I spent a lot of time in Germany at that point of my career, I decided to attempt to learn German. I began to be successful. I began to be able to speak basic German, and I began to be able to understand some of what others were saying when I was there. I cared. I wanted to learn and began to learn.

I learned words and phrases; although I was probably as talented as a three-year-old German child, I was learning. I was excited, and I wanted to learn more. Each day, I was eager to learn something new. If I had been immersed into the language on a daily basis, I would have learned it.

However, I got a new job that reduced my trips to Germany. My trips were not as often or as long, and I was busy doing a new job with new priorities and new things to learn. Two years went by before I needed to go back to Germany. Guess what? I remembered some words and phrases, but I was no longer able to speak even basic things. I wasn't able to understand as much. I had lost much of what I had gained in a short period of time. With the change of jobs, I had lost my desire to learn German. I had failed to devote the time to the subject. Essentially, I had lost my reason to care; as a result, it was no longer something

I developed or spent time on. If I want to get it back, I know what I need to do. The question always comes down to what you spend your time on and what you care about. The same is true for LeadeReliability.

Simply talking about minimizing the impact of unplanned events will continuously raise the awareness around the benefits of doing it and will keep the topic of unplanned events at the forefront of your mind.

ACCOUNTABILITY

Ask the members of your organization, family, or group, "How many people think we should have more unplanned events?" I am confident the response will be none. No one would want an increase in the number of unplanned events because we all know that unplanned events disrupt our professional and personal lives. Academically, everyone agrees that unplanned events should be eliminated.

Some people say, "No, I don't think there should be more unplanned events. Someone should do something about that!"

Unplanned events are always someone else's problem when you don't take ownership of them. If they are considered a normal occurrence of everyday life and can't be avoided, they become accepted.

People need to say, "I need to do something about this." They need to take action. Everyone can do something about everything to some degree—if they decide they want to. The point is that they need to decide. They need to discover their own reason why they would care to do something about it and in essence change their academic understanding of the situation into a passionate concern. The journey from the head to the heart is a long one that allows the development of personal accountability around LeadeReliability, which allows the journey to begin.

There is a difference between academic understanding and passion that captures the heart. As I said before, my history teacher helped create my interest in history. Why can one person not be interested in a topic at all while another is completely passionate about the topic? It is that stirring of the heart. I am not sure what about history actually captures my heart, but I know exactly how it feels. Think of something you care about. I have visited forts, cathedrals, battlegrounds, cemeteries, national monuments, and places of historical significance throughout the world and have felt deeply moved by the experiences. I am a student of the American Civil War and the American civil rights movement, and my historical heroes are Martin Luther King Jr., Abraham Lincoln, and Nelson Mandela. I have sat in Christ Church Cathedral in Oxford and imagined the people who have walked in that building. I have sat in the cathedral in Strasbourg, France, and allowed the building to speak to me about its history. I have sat in the square of Antwerp, Belgium, and imagined who has walked there. I have sat in the church in Gettysburg, Pennsylvania—two rows behind where Abraham Lincoln sat—and allowed history to speak to me. I love history and am a passionate student of anything I can learn. It is something that I am passionately engaged in, and I can never get enough of it. When your heart is stirred, you know it. I know I am accountable for my own history as well. I know what I learn from history can help me in the future. Accountability results from a stirring of the heart that causes you to do something.

Proactive Behaviors

What happens when you care about something? *Managing the Unexpected* explains how to become a highly reliable organization and the behaviors of such an organization. My experience over the past twelve years shows that when an unplanned event's impact is minimized, the five behaviors described in the book are practiced.

- deference to expertise
- sensitivity to operations
- reluctance to simplify
- preoccupation with failure
- resilience

These five behaviors must be performed to minimize the impact of unplanned events. When one or all of them are ignored, the unplanned event will run its course and create as much disruption as it possibly can. If unplanned events are thought of as normal, these behaviors are not practiced. These behaviors are so powerful because they create LeadeReliability. Once an unplanned event begins to manifest itself, if these behaviors are applied, they will work to minimize the impact as much as possible.

Many unplanned events are not minimized because people do not overtly think about minimizing the impact of unplanned events or practice the behaviors. Focusing on minimizing unplanned events will lead you to those five behaviors.

Your focus on minimizing the impact of unplanned events will cause you to practice these behaviors or your translation of them. That is what is so amazing to me about the work in *Managing the Unexpected* and the nature of the behaviors required to minimize unplanned events. All five behaviors are completely self-discoverable and consistent—no matter the type of unplanned event. By minimizing unplanned events, you will start to see the impact on the situation at hand.

Throughout the world people practice a behavior over and over again and that behavior is walking down a flight or multiple flights of stairs. Most of the time, these people perform the act reliably. They successfully make it to the bottom of the stairs without being injured. Without overtly stating it, these people have committed that they will make that descent of three steps or three hundred steps safely.

What behaviors will ensure that they do it safely? Let's assume that most people who descend stairs have not read Dr. Weick and Dr. Sutcliffe's book and know nothing about those behaviors. What will they do to ensure that they descend the stairs safely? LeadeReliability is how you do it—and not what you do. What they are doing is walking down the steps; how they do it will determine if they constantly and consistently meet their commitments.

Those who are focused on LeadeReliability will first believe that it is possible to fall down the steps. If you believe you could fall, you will be preoccupied with failure. If this behavior does not exist, many of the other behaviors will not develop, and the chance of doing it safely becomes a bit lower. Assuming our "stair descender" has the "believe I could fall" behavior, what comes next? The person will instantly look for a way to make the descent more safely.

The next thing they will do is try to remember how they have descended flights themselves or have seen others descend safely in the past. They will practice the behavior by remembering how to descend safely (deference to expertise). They will hold the handrail or pay more attention if no handrail exists. Those who weren't preoccupied with failure will begin their descent without regard for either.

After they have thought about the handrail—if there is one—and they are completely reliable, they will grab the handrail for support (reluctance to simplify). If there is not one, they will choose another path that has one or will begin the descent in a deliberate and careful fashion, holding on to anything that will give them additional support or balance. Those who are not completely reliable, even though the handrail is there, will ignore it and begin the descent. If they stumble, the rest will be left to chance.

The people who grab the handrail may have stumbled and caught themselves before and prevented a fall or tumbled down the steps because they were not holding the handrail. They may have heard of someone who has fallen and decided they don't want to repeat it. They are practicing resilience because falling down steps is not fun.

You can see the simplest activity can be done unreliably or with LeadeReliability. What you are doing doesn't change—but how you are doing it does.

Although the five behaviors are clearly defined by Weick and Sutcliffe, what you call those behaviors doesn't really matter. Discovering what they mean to you does. I have discovered that people who focus on minimizing unplanned events discover what these behaviors truly mean and translate them into their own language. They apply them to minimize unplanned events. The five behaviors are universal; understanding how they impact you and how you work allows you to change your knowledge of them from academic to passionate.

LEARN AND THEN SHARE YOUR KNOWLEDGE.

Once you do something, you have the ability to learn. If I pour myself a cup of coffee, I know how hot it is by touching the cup. I get further information about the temperature and its aroma as I bring it closer to my mouth. My knowledge about the cup of coffee grows as it gets closer to my lips. The translation of that knowledge and my past experience will determine whether I take a sip. If I do, another bit of knowledge is gained about the temperature and the flavor. Some of the learning is deliberate and some is subconscious, but we are always processing information and learning from it. We do some things with the intent to learn, but it isn't always top of mind. What we do with what we learn is the most important.

Most people apply what they learn and stop there. Although this is a good thing, it is only a small amount of the potential learning they could have. Your learning can have exponential impact if you share what you learn with others. There are two ways to learn—we can teach ourselves or be taught by others. If people don't share what they know with others, the only way for those people to learn about the topic is to learn it for themselves or find someone who is willing to teach them. By not teaching and sharing our learning with others, the extra value that our learning can generate is eliminated. People do not share their knowledge with others for a number of reasons. These reasons make a huge difference in how people perceive the concept of teaching.

I didn't know I should teach. Everyone should share what they know with others. It makes up 50 percent of the way people learn and is an incredible way for each of us to learn more. Make it a well-known fact and tell those in your organization to share what they know with others and reward them for the behavior when they do.

I don't know how to teach. Our definition of teaching is sharing what you know with others; it does not seem to be a daunting task. When people think of teaching, they conjure up images of an expert in a subject relaying expertise to others so they can achieve some proficiency in the subject. In LeadeReliability, teaching means sharing experiences and learning—and everyone has an opportunity to do it. Every person has a wealth of knowledge and experience. Sharing it is an incredibly unselfish act, and the person sharing the knowledge typically learns even more from the opportunity too.

What I know is not worth teaching. How do you know? The only way to discover if your knowledge and experience is worthwhile is to share it with another. If you don't, you will never know what opportunities and enhancements were missed. In my mind, failure to share knowledge and experiences with others is a selfish decision. Without sharing, it is impossible to know the impact the knowledge and experience could have had. The value of that knowledge and experience is suppressed and not given a chance to create more value. Knowledge and experience are free gifts that one person can give to another. That piece of knowledge—or the learning from that experience—could be the key for another to make a significant contribution.

If I keep my knowledge to myself, I will be important and powerful. Knowledge kept to yourself is valuable for a small amount of time, but shared knowledge creates importance and power. If you keep your knowledge to yourself to gain power, you will ultimately lose it. If you keep your knowledge to yourself, you eventually will become irrelevant. Sharing your knowledge creates power and relevance for you. To prove how impactful the willingness to share knowledge is, try an experiment.

The next time you set out to learn something, pick three individuals with whom you will share the knowledge you learn. You will discover how much differently you will learn. If you are learning for yourself and for others, you will put much more effort and energy into the learning process. You will pay much closer attention to what is being taught, and you will learn to share the information with someone else. The process will benefit your learning and comprehension. If you don't understand, you will ask questions. You will immerse yourself in the learning so you can share it with others. Those you teach will be able to do something else while you are learning. If you really want to gain power and importance, teach and share what you know with others. People desire to be with someone they can learn from. The more you learn to share with others, the more you will learn—and the more others will desire to be with you.

I don't have time to teach. This is probably the biggest reason people give for not teaching, and it is a self-fulfilling prophesy. When someone needs to repeat a task, there is no one else to do it because he or she has not taught anyone else. A person who has enough of these activities can be completely consumed by them and never create the time or space to do anything else. Teaching by sharing knowledge is the only way I know to create time.

Learning in order to Teach

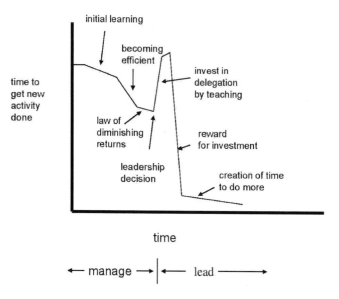

It requires a brave decision to share what is known with others because it takes additional time, at first, to do it. That time is really an investment in the other person as well as in yourself. If the time is not taken to teach, then that person always must do the task. If time is invested in teaching someone else, then the next time the task needs to be done, that person can do it—and the teacher can spend the time doing something else.

Teaching is a brave leadership decision, but it is what all great leaders do. This is a prime example of where leading differentiates itself from managing. Managers repeat tasks and become proficient at doing them, but they always must do them. When leaders allow someone else to learn how to do a task, it is a chance for the leader to do something else. Also the talents of the other person could possibly allow the task to be done better. Leaders teach, and teachers lead.

Don't misinterpret sharing of knowledge and empowerment to do a task as giving away the responsibility for the results. If you are ultimately responsible for the outcome, you may still need to stay involved, but your time will be greatly reduced. This will allow time to be impactful in other areas.

Leadership allows you to do something else while a task is completed.

One of my passions is horses. I care for eight Arabian horses, and this is one of the joys of my life. During the winter months, I put my horses in the barn at night to feed them and keep them out of the weather and the wind. Every morning, I turn them out to a fresh supply of hay disbursed throughout the pasture. During the night, the horses eat and stay out of the elements. They also allow nature to take care of things; when they leave, the eight of them have left healthy deposits of recycled hay that must be removed from their stalls.

I am kind of fussy about the cleanliness of the horse stalls, and I do a thorough job of cleaning and refreshing the stalls. After twenty years, I am pretty good at the task—possibly an expert. Horses are a passion, but they are not my profession. My profession causes me to travel periodically, but the stalls still need to be taken care of every morning. How can I travel and still get the horses taken care of? I have shared what I want done with the horses with someone else—and he does it. in my absence. This allows me to be confident that the task gets done as well as—or better than—I do it. I have the freedom to spend time on another passion, my profession. At the ranch, I manage the task. When I am traveling, I lead it.

Be brave and unselfish and share your knowledge with others!

The cycle continues. Once knowledge is shared with someone else, awareness is raised for that person. Possibly the very thing that person learned will allow him or her to develop a reason to care and become more passionate about LeadeReliability. As new information is gathered and learning occurs, everyone can validate it to ensure that the alignment still makes sense. Once knowledge is shared and learning occurs, the abilities of individuals and the organization are enhanced. Once someone new becomes aware, the cycle continues—one person at a time.

Each time someone goes through the cycle, he or she can impact another person. After numerous times, the culture will be impacted. Although it occurs one heart at a time, the more hearts and different reasons to care about the alignment that are developed, the greater the chance that someone else will be positively impacted. As each person is persuaded to develop a reason to care, the alignment is confirmed and the ability to minimize the impact of unplanned events is raised.

Leadership

With each new heart, the culture takes one step further down the LeadeReliability path. Awareness will continue to grow, and more individuals will take the personal accountability to minimize the impact of unplanned events.

The newly converted hearts will say, "I need to do something about minimizing the impact of unplanned events." And they will take action. With every action, new learning occurs. These individuals know they should share what they know. They will share what they know. The cycle moves forward one person at a time.

PATIENCE

Jean-Jacques Rousseau said, "Patience is bitter, but the fruit is sweet."

You are changing the culture. After alignment, ability, awareness, personal accountability, proactive behaviors, learning, and teaching, you will need patience. Since the change happens one person at a time, it takes time. Just as you developed your own reason to care about LeadeReliability, each individual in the organization must develop their reason to care. Some make the transition and move toward personal reliability very quickly, but it takes time for others. It could take years! Where your culture starts—and how far it is from LeadeReliability—will determine how the culture will transition.

Wherever the culture starts, it is usually firmly established. The challenge is to create enough momentum to get it moving. It will typically take months to develop the activation energy necessary to get the culture moving. The speed in which progress is made will be based on the desire of the individuals involved and how quickly they develop compelling reasons to become personally reliable. The culture is not established until the tipping point is reached and the majority is on board.

The other issue is distraction. To create awareness, you have to talk about it all the time. Until LeadeReliability is firmly established as a way of life in the culture, talking about it all the time is imperative. If distractions, which come in many forms, become the focus of the efforts, they will replace any focus on LeadeReliability. Since the focus is on the distraction and not on LeadeReliability, distraction will become the center of the new culture. You will focus on something other than minimizing the impact of unplanned events. The abnormal state of accepting unplanned events as something inevitable will become normal again—and you will go back to however the old culture treated them.

Once the distraction occurs, instead of allowing it to become the focus, figure out how you can use LeadeReliability as the answer to the problems the distraction creates and continue to focus on minimizing the impact of unplanned events rather than the distraction. Here is an example of how distractions can occur—and how moving toward reliability can be the correct approach.

A distraction is focusing on cutting costs instead of focusing on reliability. In today's turbulent economy, regional, geographic, and global economic turmoil is prevalent. Cutting costs can be an apparent solution for any economic problem. Depending on your organization's financial health, you may have to manage your costs to survive if LeadeReliability doesn't exist.

If the cutting-costs lever is pulled every time there is economic turmoil, there will be no progress. The organization will be stuck applying the same solution to every problem and never moving forward. Remember the definition of insanity—doing the same thing over and over and hoping for a different result. Success will continue to cycle around some midpoint and never really move away from there. Results will maintain the status quo.

There are actions that could be taken that would lead to LeadeReliability. Focus on minimizing the impact of unplanned events through personal reliability must continue to develop and advance. If the distraction becomes such a fixation, restarting is impossible or severely delayed. If there is a continued focus on reliability and minimizing the impact of unplanned events, this will free up resources. These resources can be targeted at further increases in reliability. The momentum and realization will capture new hearts and raise awareness, and the culture will continue to spiral positively.

If the culture focuses on costs—and it becomes the only point of conversation—then poor reliability decisions will undoubtedly be made. LeadeReliability will no longer be the focus, and the quest for reliability driven by leadership will spiral down for the foreseeable future.

Patience is a key to cultural transition and success. Jean-Jacques Rousseau said, "The fruit is indeed very sweet."

CULTURAL COMPARISON

Who should you compare yourself to? When a culture begins to change, there is a desire to determine how successful the transition is. Oftentimes a big mistake is made when trying to determine this success. This mistake is trying to compare the changing culture with another culture to see if the change is progressing fast enough. This is a huge mistake! Every culture is unique. So the only culture that you can compare progress against is the culture that is being left behind and not someone else's culture. The culture change is happening one heart at a time.

When a new individual in the culture decides to care, the culture takes a step forward. This culture is changing—not another one. How do you compare yourself to yourself? Metrics are a good way to quantify the change, and it is important to establish metrics that matter. These will be discussed later in the book.

The good news is that cultural change is often occurring before the metrics move. This is often a frustrating time for those who want to see the change. This is another reason some abandon the effort and drift back to the old culture. To prevent this from happening, I recommend describing the existing culture before the culture change gets started. Develop a one-page description of how the existing culture constantly and consistently meets its commitments and minimizes the impact of unplanned events.

After the snapshot of the state of LeadeReliability is captured, put the description in a safe place and don't look at it. When the time comes and frustration takes over because the metrics are not moving fast enough and progress seems too slow, pull out the original description to see how far the LeadeReliability needle has moved. In most cases, the progress will be much more than you thought. Then describe the present culture again in terms of LeadeReliability and celebrate all the change that has taken place. Put the new description away for another day. The amount of movement in the culture will be enough to get rid of the frustrations and keep the journey moving forward until the metrics finally move. It will take a majority demonstrating LeadeReliability to move the metrics, but the subtle changes captured in your descriptions will happen almost immediately.

This journey is hard, but the value will be evident and measurable.

CHAPTER 7

ROLE OF LEADERSHIP

A genuine leader is not a searcher
for consensus but a molder of consensus.
—Martin Luther King Jr.

In the last chapter, we discussed the essentials for change and executing a culture. I have alluded to the need for leadership, and there is nothing more correct than that statement. From the name, the importance of leadership in LeadeReliability is obvious. Without it—first from one person and then from the entire organization—LeadeReliability will never occur. Leadership at all levels is essential to success.

If you look at any website about leadership, you will find hundreds of quotes about leadership.

Effective leadership is not about making speeches or being
liked; leadership is defined by results not attributes.
—Peter Drucker

A leader is best when people barely know he exists, when his work
is done, his aim fulfilled, they will say: we did it ourselves.
—Lao Tzu

> Leadership is the art of getting someone else to do
> something you want done because he wants to do it.
> —Dwight D. Eisenhower

When it comes to LeadeReliability, what is leadership? Where can you find it? As you will see in the diagram discussed in the last chapter, leadership shows up in many places.

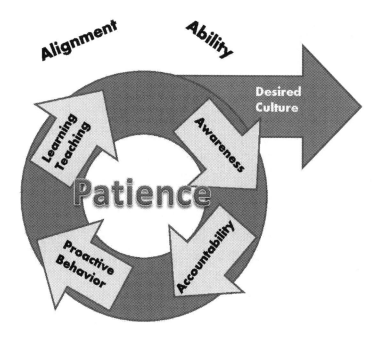

ALIGNMENT

It takes a leader to initiate alignment and set the direction and course. Whether this is at the family level or at the multibillion-dollar corporate level and all places in between, someone must take a leadership position and decide where the organization is headed. What does the desired culture look like—and what path will the organization take to get there?

Ability

Leadership shows itself here if a person decides to use ability to move the alignment forward. The leader can do an initial evaluation of the strengths and weaknesses of the organization to allow it to begin the journey toward what is desired.

Awareness

Leaders talk about what matters to many people in the organization. Leaders talk about what matters to them. We care about what we talk about; the only way to raise awareness for others is if the leaders talk about what they care about all the time. That is what leaders do.

Accountability

Leaders say, "I need to do something."

They do not idly sit back and wait for others to take action. Leaders take the initiative to get involved and get in position to do things themselves. If the alignment is sound, no one will dispute that it should be done. If leaders really care about something, they will quickly realize that they have to engage to make it happen.

Proactive Behaviors

Leaders are proactive—not reactive. They think about what they will do before they need to do it. They think ahead and develop strategy and plans for success—and contingencies if the plans don't work out. They think about the signs of success and failure—and plan what they will do if either occurs.

Teaching

If you take away anything from this book, I would ask you to take away at least this one nugget. Leaders teach. We discussed all the reasons that people may not teach. Leaders learn with the intent of sharing with others—and that is what they do with everything they learn. Leaders teach what they learn by testing it and experimenting with it. Most of all, they share it openly and broadly with others.

Patience

Leaders are patient with continuously moving plans forward and not changing with every turn and twist of the outside world. Managers react and change the path. Leaders are patient and know where they are going—and they continue in that direction regardless of interruption or detour.

Colin Powell said, "Leadership is the art of accomplishing more than the science of management says is possible."

General Powell immediately notices and projects that leadership and management are different things. He does not define one as good or one as bad, but he does imply that one is free and changing while the other is much more stagnant and fixed. He makes the point that leadership has the possibility to drive and deliver more than management can. Let's look at the two words he uses. No not leadership and management—but art and science.

What is art?

Is this art? Many of you would say no, but some would say yes. What does that tell us about art? Art is defined by the person—and not by some methodology or fixed formula. It is available and definable by every person. We each have our own definitions of art. We can develop our own definitions of leadership and determine what it means for each of us. Art is not arguable or definable—we can define what we think art is. It is actionable and always changes. It is not static. Art is not created unless someone does something. Art requires action, and leadership requires action. Leadership is defined by the individual—and is unique to the individual—and requires action.

Science is a constant, known, and measured discipline until it is proven wrong. Science can change, but only with significant breakthroughs. Oftentimes, once science is defined, it is accepted and not challenged. Science exists without action. If I hold an object in my hand five feet from the floor and let it go, what is known? The object will fall and accelerate toward the floor at roughly thirty-two feet per second squared. This will happen every time you drop the object. We know it to be a fact—and we know that part of science will never change. What does this say about management if it is like science? It must be definable, measurable, and exist whether action is taken or not. It is always the same.

Remember those horses and the "recycled grass" they leave for me each morning. I decided the stalls needs to be cleaned on a daily basis. Cleaning the stalls is a managed task. It is definable—and its success can be measured. The task is there to be done each morning—and it is very much the same each time.

Some of what we do must be managed to accomplish it, but many of the things we do can be done through leadership. The issue is that we often manage the things we should lead. Leadership and management are not good or bad but they are different.

KNOWLEDGE AND LEADERSHIP

Knowledge is a powerful, important concept, and it should never be treated as a constant. Facts are constant and are a basis of knowledge, but knowledge is not stagnant. Knowledge is defined as information and skills acquired through experience or education. This definition—like General Powell's comment about leadership—implies dynamic change. Acquired means action must be taken; with education and experience, there is always more to learn and experience. If you treat knowledge as constant and stagnant, you will stop learning—and your knowledge will be outdated.

Daniel Boorstin, the former librarian of Congress, said, "The great obstacle to discovering the shape of the earth, the continents, and oceans was not ignorance but the illusion of knowledge." He was telling us to be careful because knowledge may be a huge obstacle to discovering new things. If you treat knowledge as stagnant or as fact, you no longer think it is necessary to learn. Knowledge becomes science that you believe must be proved wrong. What does this say about leaders and managers when it comes to knowledge?

Leaders act differently than managers do when knowledge is concerned. Managers typically learn so that they know. Once they know, they can use that knowledge in a task. They are involved and direct an activity. Leaders often learn so they can share what they have learned with others; in turn, they are able to test that knowledge against the knowledge of others. If you think you already know something, there is nothing left to learn or test. If you learn something and test it with others, you will determine if it is true for now or not knowledge at all. You will not make the assumption that your knowledge is fact. Some knowledge is fact—but not all.

The only way to test your knowledge is to share it, discuss it, determine if it is true, and decide how much more there is to learn. Don't allow your knowledge to block your discovery of new knowledge. Allow knowledge to be the beginning and not the end.

Remember our nugget—leaders teach and share their knowledge with others.

Leaders learn to share what they know with others because they realize that knowledge kept to themselves has some value, but knowledge shared with others can be tested and discussed. This creates additional value. If a person takes the approach that the more he or she learns, the more they share with others, they will soon learn that the combined knowledge grows. If that person holds the knowledge to themselves, only they can add to it. Many managers use knowledge so they can do—or direct—something better. They use it to do things more efficiently, but they are involved. They become experts at doing something and telling others how to do it. There is nothing wrong with this approach, but you can see how it is less effective because it deals with the thoughts and ideas—and testing of one person rather than a group.

Choosing Leadership

There are typically two types of people in the world; each day, we get to choose which one we will be. One is more likely to lead because they learn to share knowledge. The other gathers knowledge but decides what is important and often fails to teach. You decide which way you act and what conditions cause you to act one way or the other.

The first person believes he or she has defined what there is to know to be successful and sets off to learn it. They work hard at learning it and continue to learn until they have really mastered it; at some point, this person thinks they know everything.

Do you ever think you know everything or know someone who does? Think of some words that you would use to describe a person who thinks they know everything. Arrogant might come to mind. Strong-willed, if not headstrong, could be another description. Opinionated and prejudiced might be others. How willing are these people to teach and share knowledge with others? Do they freely share with the expectation of learning more—or do they normally spend most of their time telling what they know to a select group of people or sharing their knowledge only when asked?

The start for the second person is not much different; he or she defined what there is to know to be successful. The similarities end there. This person discovers when they learn something that their view was too narrow. They discover immediately that there is so much more to learn. The process of seeking more knowledge validates how much more there is to learn. They realize that what there is to learn is expansive, and soon this person begins to believe that they don't know anything—even though they have acquired vast knowledge. This person is always learning and sharing what they have learned with others. As a result of this sharing, they are refining their knowledge even more.

What words would you use to describe this type of person? I often hear of an open-minded personality. Eager, energetic, humble, and confident are other descriptions. How willing is this person to share their knowledge? How broad is the group they are willing to share the knowledge with?

Those who fall into the trap of thinking they know everything do so because they have decided what is important to know. Those with a vast amount of knowledge who still understand how much more there is to know are always broadly seeking that knowledge for themselves and from others. If you had to pick one of these people to be a leader and one to be a manager, which person would you pick for which role? The person who is broadly seeking knowledge all the time would be the leader.

Managers spend a lot of their time perfecting what they need to know to be successful in a target area and become experts and efficient at creating that space. They become really good at what they do and often prove their expertise and value for their efforts. Even though they typically create value in their areas of expertise or operation, oftentimes their range of influence and expertise is defined and limited. Experts and people who do specific things very well are essential to organizational success, but it is imperative that these people don't allow their predefined knowledge to trap them into stagnation and make them irrelevant.

Leaders, on the other hand, spend a lot of time discovering what they don't know and dialoguing about their discoveries with others. This allows the people the leader is conferring with to respond and react with knowledge and ideas to create value as well. This open dialogue allows them to express their ideas and create more value than if the dialogue was closed and the leader told others specifically what to do. More often than not, the leader is setting direction and creating space for others to learn and develop. The leaders realize the importance of expertise and allow those more knowledgeable than themselves to make the decisions. At the same time, they encourage the experts to continue to broaden their views so they can lead through expertise.

Each day you get to choose who you will be. Do you have a targeted amount to learn? Are you becoming satisfied that you are becoming really good at it? Do you know that learning opens you to realizing how much there is left to learn? You will never come close to learning it all. Leaders never stop learning since they realize learning more helps them to help others.

What Is a Leader?

The leader is an artist who has decided what path leadership will take him or her down. Along the way, they share their learning and knowledge with whomever will listen. They always say, "I need to do something," and they always do it. Nike advertisements say, "Just do it!" And that is what leaders do. In every situation, leaders decide what action they should take—and they do it.

Once they do something, they learn from what they have done. After analyzing the action, they deliver the ultimate gift of leadership. They share what they have learned with others. They teach because they want to—and because they *have* to. It is an important part of what they do as leaders. Knowledge has a benefit for one person, but what it holds for a group of people can be immeasurable. Knowledge has so much more potential if it is shared broadly. We have to convince every person to share those rewards with everyone else when they uncover the treasure of knowledge. We can only learn in two ways. We can learn for ourselves or from others. The more there is sharing of knowledge broadly, the more impactful that knowledge can become.

Every person can choose to lead—no matter what their position, background, or education. Every person can choose to be a leader—no matter where he or she is in life. Whether you are a homemaker, a CEO, a craftsperson, a student, a player on a sports team, or a person who does manual labor for a living, you can lead.

Being a leader requires action and intention. Leadership is purposeful and does not wait for the right time. Leadership is constant and growing.

- Leaders know they should lead.
- Leaders are intentional.
- Leaders use their existing knowledge and experience to take action.
- Leaders create awareness.
- Leaders always say, "I need to do something."
- Leaders do it.
- Leaders learn.
- Leaders teach and share knowledge.
- Leaders capture hearts because people love to learn and be taught.
- Leaders have passion for what they believe in.

If a group of people is interested in minimizing the impact of unplanned events, leadership will bring LeadeReliability to the organization. LeadeReliability is unachievable without leadership!

CHAPTER 8

WE ARE ALREADY RELIABLE

Only a mediocre person is always at his best.
—W. Somerset Maugham

Whenever you broach the topic of reliability, you hear that we don't really have to worry about reliability because we are already reliable enough. You hear about all the hard work that is being done, which is another reason not to worry about reliability. I have even heard it said that we know reliability is important, but we are just too busy to work on it.

By seeking LeadeReliability, the implication is not that the organization is unreliable. All organizations are reliable to some degree—or they would not be successful at what they do. If they were unreliable, they would most likely be out of business. It is not a measure of unreliability, but the premise is that the organization is not as reliable as it could be. The level of reliability that an organization has attained without consciously trying to minimize the impact of unplanned events has been successful to a degree, but it has wasted time and resources. In some cases, the waste is more than is affordable. No matter the economic climate, the waste of time and resources is never a good thing. It can lead to customer disappointment and employee dissatisfaction that the organization doesn't need to deal with.

The second point is that all work does not necessarily translate into productivity or reliability. Many people and organizations are busy—but not necessarily productive—and some are reliable. The further the culture is from LeadeReliability, the more work that is nonproductive. Work sometimes is the wrong thing a person or group should be doing. Sometimes pausing and considering what needs to be done and planning what to do next is much more productive than just doing something and seeing if it works. Not doing anything is sometimes the most productive and reliable thing to do. If the notion of focusing on productivity is something that hasn't been considered by an organization, then there is a lot to explore.

LeadeReliability is the constant and consistent meeting of commitments. Is the organization as reliable as it could be? Maybe we could ask the question a little differently by asking if you are dependable enough. If you are satisfied that you are, maybe there is little for you and your organization to work on. Again, if what you are doing is not consciously attempting to minimize the impact of unplanned events and constantly and consistently meeting commitments, then there is work to do—and time and resources are being wasted.

This is where the work question comes into play. How much work do you have to do to reach a level of dependability to constantly and continuous meet your commitments to your customers and your stakeholders? How much work has to be redone or repeated to reach that level of dependability? If individuals and organizations are not able to meet their commitments without redoing things, they are not as dependable or as reliable as they could be. Your ability to minimize the impact of unplanned events is the true measure of efficiency. It starts with the individual and moves to the organization.

Let's take a look at the organization first and describe a continuum of organizations that I have run across while working in the business world. Sam McNair's fantastic work shows you the results of the various organizational efforts.

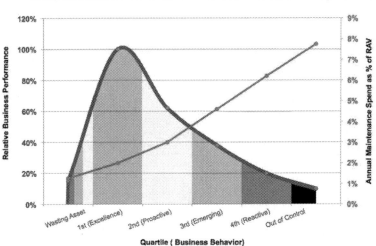

Steady State Business Performance vs. Behavior and Maintenance Spend

Relative Business Performance (RBP) is the measure of how well an organization meets its commitments. Therefore, 100 percent is achievable because even though the organization is not perfectly reliable, it is able to meet all of its commitments at the lowest cost.

The most unreliable organization in the continuum is what I call chaos. This organization is busy doing lots of work; it has more work than the organization can possibly accomplish and look like bees in a hive. Employees are constantly working, moving, and doing what they believe needs to be done. As the work is observed, you see a lack of order in what they do. They just do because they think they need to always be doing something—and that is normal for them. Trial and error is the method for accomplishing work, especially new tasks; once they make an error, they quickly move on to the next attempt to be successful. They do significant amounts of work but accomplish little; as a result, they are forced to work even more and longer to achieve success.

McNair's benchmarking suggests that this type of culture (out of control) achieves less than 20 percent RBP compared to LeadeReliability, which achieves 100 percent because it meets all its commitments. Chaos culture also spends three times as much on resources to create their level of RBP. It costs three times more to deliver five times less reliability. In the chaos culture, significant work can occur with little output.

Chaos and LeadeReliability have high levels of freedom to act—and different results. As the notion of reliability starts to gain traction, chaos culture gains a little order and becomes active. Active can be thought of as structured chaos. The organization is beginning to add structure and process to the work it does. Individuals fill the roles with a level of chaos—and some added structure. As you move out of chaos into active, structure begins and some freedom to act must be taken away. Freedom to act is always desirable. If the culture is moving to a more desirable state, why is there less freedom to act? As we walk through the cultural transition, it will become clear how the freedom to act is regained. Remember our discussion on managing and leading? To move from chaos to active, it requires more management of activity and less individual freedom to act. Later leadership replaces management, and individual freedom to act is restored. It grows as leadership replaces managing.

In the active culture, structure takes shape, which is good, but typically the structure begins to morph into territory or silos. If the silos and territories become too guarded, they create a level of inefficiency. The attempt to bring order also often creates boundaries. These boundaries are not always intentional, but they develop nonetheless. People focus on their areas of responsibility—but there is some chaos. The one positive thing that chaos has, freedom to act, is reduced as structure develops. The structure leads to the creation of boundaries, which is beneficial unless those boundaries create silos. McNair discovered that through the creation of structure these cultures (which he calls reactive) increase RBP slightly to 20 percent and reduce the cost to create reliability by a small percentage.

Reactivity follows activity and creates more structure and a focus on delivering on commitments. Since there is still a lot of reworking—and most of the work involving the handling of issues occurs after the unplanned events have already occurred—reliability and dependability are not achieved. Systems are put in place to respond to things that go wrong; because systems are put in place, more things go right than in the previous two cultural organizations. Still there is a significant amount of things that can go wrong. This is when organizational silos and barriers become strongest.

Departments and groups claim their areas of expertise and oftentimes work exclusively in these areas of focus. If cross-functional work and idea exchange does not develop, then groups and functions will only worry about their areas of expertise and become very protective of these areas. As a result they will rarely take input from outside the group. Small fiefdoms are created inside the organization with very little cross-fertilization of ideas and initiatives. Internal competition between functions can draw more attention than making progress against external competitors. These cultures typically have the lowest amount of freedom to act because the work processes and methods are prescriptive to rid the organization of chaos. There is a lot of direction given to employees in these cultures.

Managers thrive in these types of cultures because they have their hands in much of the work and employees wait for the managers to tell them what to do before they act. Managers are rewarded for how much they know about the daily routines and activities. There is a lot of pressure put on the managers to create success; since they can't be in all places all the time, many unplanned events happen and are dealt with after the fact. These cultures have structure that adds to reliability, but the decisions are left to the managers. What Sam McNair discovered in this culture (which he calls emerging) is that the added structure has a positive impact on RBP and the cost to create reliability. RBP is twice as good as it is in chaos—at 45 percent of the cost.

If the organization does not become enamored with allowing managers to be in charge—and unsatisfied with unplanned events being a normal part of work—then the focus begins to shift toward becoming more reliable and more proactive. I call this culture proactive—as does Mr. McNair. Proactive cultures anticipate issues and solve them before the unplanned events have significant impact. There still are unplanned events that are addressed in a reactive mode, but more are addressed before any damage can be done. This is the birth of reliability and the beginning of the real journey toward LeadeReliability. Organizations anticipate that things can and do go wrong. They begin looking for signs of abnormalities and take action before any incidents occur.

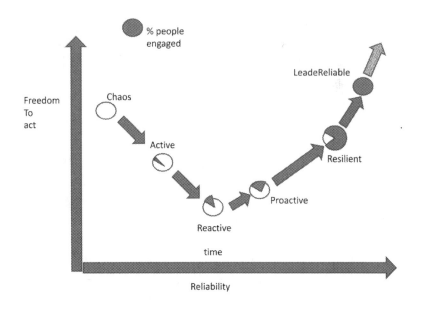

JEFF DUDLEY

They are beginning to minimize the impact of unplanned events. Silos and functional boundaries weaken. The organization begins to realize that each function needs each other to be successful. The walls are not broken down, but they are less guarded and the cross exchange of ideas begins to move in a positive direction. A leader who allows others in the organization to make decisions starts to be recognized as successful.

The days of rewarding extreme micromanagement are gone. Micromanaging still exists, but it is not the only recognized leadership style. There is still the functional rivalry, but it is less than it was. There are times when the proactive behaviors drive cross-functional success and administrative leaders reward the teamwork. The realization that everyone is on the same team begins to develop. The proactive culture truly is the birthplace where the journey toward LeadeReliability becomes serious.

Unfortunately, this is where many cultures stall on the journey toward being reliable. They become satisfied with being reliable enough. They are being proactive and positively impacting some percentage of the unplanned events; because it is so different than reactivity, they think they have achieved LeadeReliability. Unfortunately, there are still many significant unplanned events that can occur at this point. There are distinct pockets of success, but being reactive is still an accepted practice. There is still some degree of normalcy and acceptance of unplanned events. The tipping point of the cultural change has not occurred, and the majority of people haven't developed a reason to care. They see the benefit of being reliable and agree conceptually, but that acknowledgement is quickly followed by the statement that someone should do something about it—because it is not their area of focus. It is the comfort trap. The organization isn't unreliable, and it is now much more reliable than it was in the previous culture segments. Because of the progress and the ability to show when the impact of unplanned events has been minimized, they are anxious to declare victory. As the organization moves

102

through this stage, more individuals and groups say, "I need to do something about minimizing the impact of unplanned events."

The organization gets closer to the tipping point, which is where it can become much more reliable. RBP and the cost of creating reliability are positively impacted.

I call the period past the tipping point—and through the capture of the early majority's hearts—resilience. Resilience is the ability to recover from or adjust to misfortune and change. This is a big step for the organization and requires a number of dynamics to take place before an organization can approach this phase. The magnitude of effort to get from proactive to resilience is one that most organizations never achieve. They are complacent and satisfied with being proactive—or they just aren't brave and patient enough to continue the journey.

Minimizing the impact of unplanned events and constantly and consistently delivering on your commitments, has to become how the organization does everything. With every action, initiative, and behavior, every member of the organization must attempt to minimize the impact of unplanned events. They have to understand what unplanned events are doing to the organization—and they have to minimize the impact when they occur. They have to learn from them and put in mechanisms so they never occur again.

The focus on what could go wrong and preparation for the possibility that it may come to fruition are a constant part of planning. They have detected what the early signs of abnormal will look like and know exactly how they will react to minimize the impact of any unplanned event should those signs come true. They know this behavior will prevent the potential disruption of their organization—internally and externally. The organization is not perfect, especially early in this stage. Additional individuals in the organization will constantly discover what captures their hearts, and they will participate in this cultural movement. Viral, contagious, and exponential are words that describe the desire to become more reliable.

Tangible results will be delivered by the culture. Margins will increase. There will be more time to plan, do, check, and act. There will be more time to innovate and more time to think. There will be less wasted time and resources. Employees and customers will be more highly engaged and much more satisfied. Functional walls and silos will disappear, and people will act and react to any situation that looks to be abnormal. They will build in contingency to ensure success, and they will recapture the freedom to act. Leadership will replace managing. Leaders will develop throughout the organization. Many will realize that—no matter what position they hold in the organization—they are leaders and daily choose to take action.

History will not be repeated; it will be learned from and taught to others. The culture will be positioned to become LeadeReliable. If you look at Sam McNair's chart, I put the resilient culture at the interface of his proactive and excellence cultures. The level of RBP is close to 90 percent, and the cost to achieve this performance is a third of what it was in chaos. Resilient cultures have leaders who give employees the freedom to act and to create success.

The journey to achieve LeadeReliability will never stop. Cultures that make it that far will become their own critics. They continuously refine how they minimize the impact of unplanned events. They dig deeper, taking proactive measures to recognize them earlier. Unplanned events that previously would not have even been noticed are now top of mind and dealt with. The definition of an unplanned event continues to become refined and actions to prevent unplanned events are taken sooner than they ever were. The entire organization is on guard for the possibility that something could go wrong. Everything that is learned is shared with others who can benefit from the knowledge. Leaders are everywhere in the organization, and action is taken by all.

Constantly (all the time) and consistently (every individual) deliver on commitments. Laggards buy in or leave. The organization is not perfect because unplanned events still happen, but they are detected early enough that their impact is minimized. The cultural journey has now met a significant milestone, but it is never complete. Refining and critiquing and learning and teaching never stop. If they do, the organization will quickly spiral back in the wrong direction. At this point, maximum RBP is achieved, and there is optimal spending of resources to achieve it.

LeadeReliability is how you are doing what you are doing. The closer to LeadeReliability the culture has moved, the more everything has a complete focus on minimizing the impact of unplanned events and constantly and consistently meeting commitment to others.

The journey never ends; it only becomes more dynamic and interactive. The results will be phenomenal, and customers and employees will love every minute of it.

REWARDED BEHAVIORS IN THE CULTURAL PHASES

What behaviors are rewarded in the different cultural phases? All cultures have a reward system that is stated or inferred. What is rewarded drives those behaviors; what is not rewarded curtails those behaviors. Let's look at the type of behaviors that are rewarded in the various cultural stages. As long as behaviors continue to be rewarded, the culture will stay as it is.

Let's start with chaos. Since the culture is looking for those people who are always busy doing work, it naturally follows that the volume of work that is done is what is rewarded. Those who are the busiest get rewarded the most. Those who are the busiest and who are always doing something are thought to create exceptional value. What they are doing may not be productive or even noteworthy, but working is rewarded in chaos. Since there is not much structure in chaos, the reward type and frequency usually have a lack of consistency. In many cases, what is being done doesn't benefit the organization—and the sheer quantity of churn mixes the good and the bad results. Quantity is noticed. However, since there is a great level of freedom to act, substantial contributions may go unnoticed if they are not perceived as requiring significant quantities of work. Trivial and potentially low-value contributions may be disproportionately rewarded because they appeared to require significant work.

If the culture grows out of chaos to active, what is rewarded will also shift slightly. In an active culture, rewards are much like those in the chaos culture. Rewards are usually based on the amount of work done, but typically there are big group incentives. The entire group equally benefits or doesn't—regardless of individual contributions. This is a result of some of the structure that begins to develop in the active culture. This type of reward is utilized because large groups can be persuaded to take action and accomplish initiatives by putting a carrot in front of them. This strategy is often not successful because the carrot isn't big enough or interesting enough to entice the group since motivation is often individualized. What captures one person's heart may not interest another person.

With group rewards, group punishment is also present. The group plays it safe and doesn't extend itself enough to create success. It works hard enough to avoid being punished. The groups ebb and flow without a lot of success, and the reward strategy becomes ineffective. Since managers are beginning to surface in this culture, they often do the work for the group and don't see why they should reward the group because they did all the work.

As the culture becomes reactive, you see more structure in the rewards system. It may even become formal in nature, possibly to the point of being highly bureaucratic. Individual rewards surface but group rewards are still prevalent as well. In both

CHAPTER 9

HOW WILL I KNOW I AM STARTED DOWN THE RIGHT PATH?

Adversity is the first path to truth.
—Lord Byron

O nce the movement is started, this cultural journey will take time to get to the point where there are significant improvements and significant impact. A small step of improvement and impact happens each time people transform their academic agreement to minimize the impact of unplanned events to a passionate desire to do the same. Each individual transformation adds to the transformation of the whole. As the number of individuals grows, the impact will multiply and eventually become exponential. As we have discussed, a culture change takes time. Where the culture starts will dictate how long it takes and the amount of patience required. At times, the progress seems slow and unsteady, but there are a number of signposts along the way that are indications of the progress that is being made toward LeadeReliability.

Where you start is important.

Every culture is unique. The behaviors and nuances of the culture define its uniqueness. Cultures may be similar, but they are not identical. Where the culture starts on the continuum that was described will determine how the first steps toward LeadeReliability should be taken. Chaos to LeadeReliability is how we described the continuum—and the length of time that signposts will pop up is determined by the starting point. The closer the start is to chaos, the more dramatic the culture change will be. If you are starting at proactive or even further toward LeadeReliability, you may already be practicing some of the signposts I will describe. No matter where the journey starts, behavior change and improvement will be necessary to decrease the impact of unplanned events.

The journey can't be rushed. Unique cultures take time to change. Although the tendency will be to try to compare one culture's progress with another, the fact that they are unique makes this comparison irrelevant. The only culture that a culture can truly be compared to is its own. That is why using the written description of the starting culture mentioned in chapter 6 is so important. It is a method that allows the improving culture to be compared to the way it was at the beginning of the journey. Being involved in the changing culture on a daily basis makes it difficult to notice change. That is why this snapshot in time works so effectively to allow the improvement areas to be detected.

Organized for Success

Is the organization set up to be successful? Is it set up in some configuration that the design impedes LeadeReliability?

In the cultural continuum, we saw freedom to act first decrease from chaos to reactive and then increase as cultures moved from reactive to LeadeReliable. The ability to regain the freedom to act is important to the success of LeadeReliability. Organizational structure can either enhance or impede freedom to act.

Layered organizations with a strong command-and-control structure sometimes inhibit progress. In this type of organization, it requires most individuals to ask for approval to act. Even regulated industries figure out how to create leadership freedom within roles. There may be required checks and balances, but there also must be freedom so that individuals in the organization can make leadership decisions and say "I need to do something" and then have the freedom to do it.

If the organization is a matrix organization and strong silos have been created, there is typically a reluctance to act outside of them. If the roles inside the silos are highly structured and defined, then the case can exist where no one believes they have freedom to act outside of the structure. The culture will be stuck and won't advance So for matrix organizations it is important that freedom to act outside the functional silo is accepted and rewarded.

Organizational design can heavily impact the rate of culture change. No matter what the organizational design, flexibility is necessary so that individuals in the organization feel like they can take action if they choose to. Otherwise, significant effort and energy will be spent just getting to the proactive culture where the freedom to act begins to be revived. This journey is hard enough as it is, and if organizational design or practice prevents the freedom to act or has created that illusion, then that will first have to be addressed before any movement past a reactive culture can ever occur.

One person's action can lead to culture change.

The change of any culture starts with a person saying, "I don't agree with the way things are. I need to do something."

When Martin Luther King Jr. heard about Rosa Parks being arrested, he decided to do something about it. She should be able to sit wherever she wants. What can I do? To get people's attention, he organized a boycott of the bus system. This behavior led to the start of the American civil rights movement.

Mother Teresa said, "I am going to give wholehearted and free services to the poorest of the poor." The resulting behaviors behind this simple statement have spread to 133 other countries.

In LeadeReliability, the cultural leaders have chosen to minimize the impact of unplanned events by saying, "I need to do something," and taking proactive behaviors. They have seen how powerful their impact can be. Others will notice and follow their lead and become leaders themselves.

As these new leaders have impact, others start saying, "I need to do something" and then do it. They will minimize the impact of unplanned events. One day, every member of the organization will say, "I need to do something." No one will say, "Someone needs to do something."

Organizational leaders develop reasons to care.

For LeadeReliability to be as successful as it can be, each person must develop a reason to care. In most organizations, there are a large number of individuals who care—or at least take notice of—what the organizational leaders care about. The organizational leaders usually drive vision and priorities. When that vision and priority focuses on LeadeReliability, they make the minimization of the impact of unplanned events a priority. They talk about LeadeReliability and become accountable for constantly and consistently meeting of commitments made to each other and to their customers. They understand that the minimization of the impact of unplanned events leads to business and organizational success—and they drive it.

The culture can start from anywhere in the organization. It takes one person with enough vision and drive to use influence and passion to get the movement going. When the organizational leaders develop a reason to care, the culture development is expedited.

Language and Words

One of the first things you will notice on the journey is that language will change. People will use the word *reliability* much more and will talk about the behaviors that minimize the impact of unplanned events. Those leading the culture change will be fully engaged in trying to drive the culture toward LeadeReliability, and the words and concepts they use to explain it will be used by others. These potential converts will transfer the concepts from academic understanding to something they care about. As a result, they will use openly talk about the concepts.

Words and concepts that had not been heard outside of the cultural leader's environment will become more common in everyday conversations. Individuals whose hearts the leader has touched will change their behaviors. Unfortunately, there is another group who believes they know what the leader wants to hear and are keen to use the latest buzzwords. The difference is that their behavior shows no sign of change.

Ideally, this group realizes that LeadeReliability is a permanent culture change that will require them to change their behavior to be successful. No matter who is using the words, those who have become passionate about LeadeReliability should reinforce the use of the words. They should take every opportunity to translate the words into descriptions of behaviors that could work to minimize the impact of unplanned events. As the culture continues to change and advance, the translated concepts and behaviors will be part of the cultural journey.

Hear the words in unusual places.

The next thing that changes is where the words and concepts are discussed. At first, they will be primarily confined to those places where the culture leaders have influence. Since these leaders are initiating the culture change, it is normal for the concepts to be discussed. As the innovators and early adopters become involved, the words are heard in their circles. It is an extension of those who you would expect to be engaged and involved.

One day, the words or concepts will appear or be part of something that will be a surprise and may even seem out of place at first. The words regarding minimizing the impact of unplanned events will not be coming from familiar sources. They will be coming from somewhere or someone that will cause those already engaged to take notice. At this point, the words and ideas will be spreading to others whose hearts are being captured without the direct influence of the initial cultural leaders. This is a significant point in the journey, and the words should continue to be reinforced. The occurrence of the phenomena will become more common, and the sources of the discussion and conversation will become much wider.

The concepts and discussion will become more personalized and have the sound of ownership attached. This is a great indication that the concepts and ideas are being taken to heart— with behaviors soon to follow. The words are not just being parroted. Reinforcement of these conversations is critical at this stage. At some point, the words and concepts will become so common that they may stop being noticed.

See the behaviors.

The next signpost begins to have larger impact. The behaviors of LeadeReliability will become visible in a small population and grow as each heart is captured. Tangible examples of people taking action to minimize the impact of or avoiding unplanned events altogether will become evident. People will worry about what could go wrong and develop plans in case it does. Small abnormal occurrences will be detected, and the cause of the abnormality will be corrected. Proactive responses to small issues will become more common. Decisions will be made by the most knowledgeable people involved—and not just the highest ranks. People will take action outside their direct areas of responsibility because it is the right thing to do.

People will proactively seek abnormal situations rather than waiting for a more abnormal situation to discover them. There will be pockets where the impact of unplanned events is diminished—and people will have more time to do what they planned on doing. Initially this doesn't happen everywhere, but it does in places where people are discussing the concepts and seem to be more engaged in what they are doing. These behaviors are typically isolated to areas where the change started or areas closely connected to those areas, but occasionally it develops in other parts of the organization. This is one of the early indications that the culture may be beginning to take off.

React to the abnormal.

Every unplanned event starts because something abnormal occurs. There is some small deviation from normal—and things unravel from there. Those who focus on minimizing the impact of unplanned events are looking for the earliest indications of abnormalities—and doing something about it. The issue for organizations who have not started the journey to become LeadeReliable is that abnormal becomes normal very quickly. Without this proactive attempt to detect abnormal, it becomes normal and festers until it becomes a significant issue. If you don't believe that abnormal becomes normal quickly, is there something in your home that does not work correctly—or is broken—and your family has come to accept it as normal? Most of us are guilty of this. No matter the organization, the abnormal becoming normal is very common.

If it changes, members of the organization will become less tolerant of the abnormal; the moment something is perceived as abnormal, something will be done to address the issue. Abnormal never lingers; it is addressed immediately. Until the understanding of what is causing the abnormal to exist is figured out, it remains a priority.

This proactive behavior causes the abnormal to disappear, unplanned events to become minimized, and the journey toward LeadeReliability to move forward.

CHANGE WHAT YOU REWARD.

We discussed before how the reward system changes through various cultural states and how what is rewarded will drive behavior. At times, the reward system can drive behaviors that are undesirable. If conflicting reward systems are offered, the person will choose the reward that suits him or her best. It is imperative that the behaviors that are rewarded are the behaviors that are desired. What and who get rewarded will drive behaviors and impact how people respond to various conditions in the organization.

Conflicting reward systems can drive undesired behavior. Reward systems can drive behaviors that may be unknown and undesirable because the results are being monitored and rewarded instead of the behavior to achieve them. If this reward system is allowed to exist, the undesired behaviors could lead to disaster.

I have had the pleasure of raising four children, and they all have become very successful. When my oldest daughter was a teenager, she was the first attempt at raising her "right." My daughter's safety was paramount to me, and there were two areas where I perceived her safety was at risk—driving a car and being home by a predetermined time. I attempted to influence both.

I signed a contract with her that if she was able to drive from her sixteenth birthday to her eighteenth birthday without an accident or traffic citation, I would reward her with a substantial sum of money. This was also a way for me to avoid skyrocketing insurance premiums. To get her home at a predetermined time, she was given a curfew of midnight.

I drove with her, and she was a responsible, safe driver. Her desire to get the money on her eighteenth birthday caused her to drive the same way when I wasn't there. For the curfew, she had stellar performance as well. She was a safe driver and responsibly met the curfew—at least that is what the results indicated. I never really questioned the behavior that allowed her to create positive results. That ultimately was a huge mistake on my part. If I look at the two objectives, safe driving was by far the most important. However, its consequences were uncertain. Meeting the curfew was much more immediate and certain and was easily measured. Being home on time could be tracked. Getting a ticket or being in an accident, which could have had much worse consequences, would have been a onetime event. My concern was her safety.

My daughter was disciplined and never missed her curfew. On nights when she wanted to stay out until the curfew, she got home between 11:45 and 11:59. She never missed a curfew and she received her reward at eighteen. I was so proud of her because she was always home by midnight and she was a "safe" driver. Her immediate reward was making it home by midnight so she would not get in trouble with her parents. The longer-term reward was not to get in an accident or get a ticket so she could get the money. The behavior I thought I was rewarding by her meeting her curfew without exception may have been putting her at huge risk. Let's take a closer look.

The fact that she was never late says that she must have been an incredible planner. Through that planning, she was able to make it home on time every night and always drove the speed limit. Our house was on a rural road, so she had to drive on that road every night to get home by midnight—at any speed necessary to meet the curfew. This would suggest that if she was not the perfect planner, she may have taken liberty with her speed. These liberties were taken regardless of the weather conditions, the traffic conditions, or the amount of white-tailed deer and other animals along the road. She had a time to meet—and she met it. I always praised her for getting home on time and never asked her how fast she drove to accomplish that feat. While rewarding her punctuality, I was also indirectly rewarding how she did it. I would never outwardly reward her for taking liberties with the speed limit, but I had indirectly. I would never reward her for putting herself at risk while driving, but I had indirectly. At times, her unsafe driving was being rewarded immediately while I was thinking there was a strong system in place that would create safe driving habits for her.

Most organizations have some of the same reward conflicts. Are outcomes and results rewarded no matter how they are accomplished or how many resources it takes to accomplish them? Are reactions and firefighting rewarded instead of proactivity and prevention of problems altogether? What is rewarded in the organization? Until it has really been thought about, some undesired behaviors are being rewarded.

I was rewarding my daughter for breaking the speed limit and putting herself at risk. Are individuals being rewarded for coming in to save the day after the disaster has happened—or when they are proactive and prevent disasters from occurring? Are those who minimize and prevent unplanned events being rewarded?

As the culture moves toward LeadeReliability, the preventer will be rewarded instead of the repairer. The individual anticipating an issue will be rewarded and not the person who resolves it after it happens. The planner will be rewarded and not the manager of chaos. Those who constantly and consistently meet their obligations will be rewarded and not those who dramatically attempt to save the day after the commitment has been missed. Imagine your world if you reward reactions to small events rather than the drama of mopping up catastrophes. To develop a reward system that drives LeadeReliability, one like this will need to be developed.

UNPLANNED EVENTS ARE MINIMIZED— AND THE IMPACT IS NOTICED.

At first, it will be subtle and not all the dots will be connected, but as the impact of unplanned events is minimized, there are substantial positive repercussions on the performance of the internal organization and those externally impacted by it. Customers will notice that commitments made by the organization are being met more often than in the past. Employees will spend less time redoing things and dealing with someone else's emergencies. They will spend more time doing what they had planned on doing.

At this point in the journey, the number of those who care about impacting unplanned events is beginning to grow and more people are developing their personal reason to care and participate in the effort. Caring causes behaviors to have a positive impact to minimize the impact of unplanned events. Those actions can have a ripple effect on the results and the influence of others. As more people develop a personal reason to care, behaviors follow—and the positive impact happens more often. All those who benefit from the positive impact take notice. Imagine how powerful the total impact will be when everyone in the organization develops a reason to care and minimizes the impact of unplanned events. Singular influence becomes additional, then multiplied, and finally exponential.

Functional silos break down, and cross-functional solutions develop.

In large manufacturing organizations, operations and maintenance work together to resolve issues. Operations and the supply chain function work to meet customers' needs. The commercial organization and operations spend time planning the production schedule that has the most positive impact on the customer and the least waste-generation in the plant. Research and development engages operations early in the development of a project.

For a small business, the pizza driver calls back to the pizza shop to say she noticed they were getting low on boxes—and that someone should check to make sure more are on their way. The stock boy at a grocery store sees a short customer trying to maneuver a glass jar off of a higher shelf and hurries over to assist before anything breaks. At the auto repair shop, a mechanic notices a customer waiting on a salesperson and walks over to see if he can be of assistance. At home, a teenage daughter gets home after school and notices the faucet is leaking and calls a parent to see if he or she wants to try to fix it when he or she gets home—or if she should try to fix it or call the plumber.

In any type of organization, people can take action outside their primary area of responsibility. When it happens, people in the organization are starting to act like they are all on the same team and are looking at total success as the objective. They realize that any unplanned event, no matter in whose area of responsibility it occurs, will have a negative impact on the team.

Problems are addressed with cross-functional input and ideas. People solicit ideas from anyone who could have a solution to the problem—no matter what their core job is. The functional silos, especially in areas where normal collaboration makes sense, fade away.

Significant Signposts

These last two signposts are significant. They are strong signs that you are making significant progress because these two signposts are difficult. Most organizations never get to them, and they never see them practiced in the organization. Typically the journey is sidetracked or falls apart before the organization gets here—and people go back to what they have always done. They fall back to being reactive and allow what they have done in the past and the culture they are comfortable with to remain.

React to pushback and significant distractions.

There are two things that are certain to happen as your culture is developing. You will have tremendous pushback toward LeadeReliability and there will be significant distractions along the way. There will be many whose solution to both will be to continue doing what they are doing in the old culture.

All lasting cultures experience that pushback as they develop. If you could ask Nelson Mandela, Mother Teresa, Abraham Lincoln, or any other cultural change leader, they would tell you resistance is a natural part of change. The more significant the change, the more pushback the cultural change will receive.

I sometimes chuckle when I say, "Becoming more reliable will meet lots of opposition." However, it is true. Being less reliable is so much easier, and people tend to be hesitant to move away from easy. We are all reliable to some degree, but we are not as reliable as we could be. Achieving that level of reliability is the basis of the pushback. The journey toward LeadeReliability is difficult. The pushback comes from inside the organization. It comes from those who think it is okay the way it is or those who believe all the fallacies described earlier are true.

It also comes in the form of disruptions from outside the organization. Economic conditions, political disruption, customer issues, and government regulation can cause the focus to move away from reliability and toward whatever the disruption is. The culture we care about is the one we talk about. When the distraction comes, if what is talked about is the distraction rather than becoming reliable, then the distraction has won; it has become a disruption—and it will be dealt with by using the behaviors of the old culture.

What if one time you acknowledged the distraction but instead of slipping back to that old and comfortable culture to deal with the distraction, the continued pursuit of LeadeReliability was the way the distraction was dealt with. Those persistent enough to progress this far in the cultural journey and deal with this signpost will realize that no matter what the distraction, minimizing unplanned events can lead to the solution of the distraction. Here is a quick example; let's say lack of customer loyalty is the distraction. What better way is there to create customer loyalty than to constantly and consistently meet all of your commitments to them? What better way to constantly and consistently meet your commitments than to minimize the impact of unplanned events. What better way to minimize the impact of unplanned events than to create a LeadeReliability culture.

If you want brand security, customer loyalty, employee satisfaction, lower costs, and higher margins or any other need you're not meeting, LeadeReliability will deliver them. Don't allow distractions to sidetrack your journey.

PATIENCE

Culture change takes years if there has been little focus on minimizing the impact of unplanned events before. The final signpost that says you have a chance of staying on the journey is patience. Too often, organizations that start the journey toward LeadeReliability get distracted or impatient, expecting immediate results or thinking the results aren't coming fast enough.

In the early stages of the culture change, there may be early signs of progress—but that progress weakens and strengthens as the culture continues to progress. There are periods when results seem to be not improving at all. Depending on where you start your cultural journey and how heavily ingrained the old culture is, there are two phenomena you will fight against. There needs to be activation energy to get any cultural movement at all—and then there is the long road of perseverance through the various stages of cultural change. Where the journey starts will determine the length of time and effort required to change. You most likely will start with a well-established culture. The energy needed to move it can be substantial. The movement is happening one person at a time.

LeadeReliability is minimizing the impact of unplanned events. What does an unplanned event need to be minimized? It needs detection. Detection comes as a result of an individual being proactive and noticing something abnormal—and not allowing it to exist. This requires individuals to take action. Early on, if a small percentage of the organization is doing this, many unplanned events will go unnoticed—or noticed without action—and escalate into issues. The ones that are noticed are addressed and minimized. It becomes a numbers game.

The more hearts that are captured, the more proactive actions are taken, which results in more mitigation of the impact of unplanned events. The real reason for the time is how long it takes to capture a heart and then another and then another. When all the hearts are captured, the results are incredible. How long it takes can only be answered by each individual—and that takes time.

Who knows what will capture the next heart? A person will develop a personal reason to care about constantly and consistently keeping their commitments and minimizing the impact of unplanned events and will take action to make it happen.

THE JOURNEY

Signposts along the way are indications that you are on the right path. Take note of them. Some will be more substantial than others. Others may already exist or go unnoticed. This journey can feel long and difficult.

CHAPTER 10

PRIORITIZING THE WORK AND SEEING PROGRESS

> The key is not to prioritize what is on your
> schedule but to schedule your priorities.
> —Stephen Covey

The journey to LeadeReliability is common sense. There is nothing magical about the concepts and content. The issue seems easy, but not many individuals, teams, companies, organizations, or corporations act this way constantly and consistently. With every good intention, they simply fail to minimize the impact of unplanned events. The whole issue gets back to the abnormal being normal. Unplanned events are considered to be a part of normal, everyday life.

I hope you have come to the conclusion that you want to change that. If you have, then you will need to think about how you will work to make unplanned events abnormal. How will you purposefully look for abnormal and recognize how to do something about it?

Unplanned events are disruptive to your entire organization. Some are worse than others; do you know which unplanned events are the most disruptive and would have the most negative impact?

Identifying those potential unplanned events and developing a mind-set to proactively identify in all situations what abnormal looks like is the mind-set that needs to be developed. Once the mind-set is established, the next question is where to start. You can't just say, "I do not think we should tolerate any more unplanned events." You have to say, "I will not accept any more unplanned events—and I am going to do something about them."

It is best to start small with something that is important. The best time and place to start is with something that is going on today. What are the plans for today—and what will have to happen in order for those plans to be a success and not be disrupted? What will be accomplished? What will a successful day look like? If today is successful, what will you get to do that you planned on doing? If the entire day is too much to bite off, maybe you could start with the morning or the afternoon. Establish the time period and define exactly what success looks like.

What are some possible events that could occur that would prevent success for that defined time? Along those same lines, what would be the most disruptive everyday occurrence that would prevent you from experiencing perfection? This is sometimes hard to identify because of the trap of thinking that disruption is a normal part of life. Even though everyday occurrences are completely disruptive, they are still thought of as normal. Can the potential disruptions be identified?

Let's say you are planning on meeting with an important client at nine in the morning. You have been working with this client for a long time, and you are pretty sure you will close a deal to begin supplying your product. The commute to your client's office is one hour. What could you do this afternoon to ensure that tomorrow by ten o'clock you have signed the deal and been LeadeReliable? Determine what could go wrong. What could negatively impact the outcome of tomorrow?

- Your client has overbooked his day and is not available at nine.
- Your client is so excited about your product that he has decided to take more than what you thought he was going to take.
- There could be a traffic problem that will prevent you from making the commute in an hour.
- There is a power outage, and your electric alarm clock fails to go off. You oversleep and miss your appointment.
- Your car has a lingering maintenance issue that you have not addressed, and you get stranded.

Any of these five things could disrupt tomorrow. None of them are highly abnormal, but they all could happen. What can you do?

- Check with the client to make sure you are still on for nine o'clock, and let your client know how excited you are for the discussion.
- Check with your production facility to see what the maximum and minimum availability of the product is.
- Plan on arriving to your appointment early. You can always spend time in a coffee shop.
- Set a battery-powered alarm clock.
- Make sure your mode of transportation is ready to go or have a back-up plan.

These five things will help you to get to your appointment on time. Have you considered them? What will you do if your client is not ready to commit to an order yet? What plans do you have to move the relationship forward?

By thinking about these things proactively, you will have a good chance that your day will not be completely disrupted by an unplanned event.

You have practiced four of the five behaviors that lead to LeadeReliability:

- reluctance to simplify
- preoccupation with failure
- sensitivity to operations
- resilience

Any of the issues described above would not be considered abnormal, but if they disrupt what you are planning to get done with the client they are. You can proactively deal with them before they happen to prevent them from occurring or consider how to deal with them if they do. By practicing this technique, you will minimize the impact of unplanned events.

You can pick a time or an activity and plan not to let it be disrupted. How do you expand this? Every organization has a list of short-term and long-term priorities. What are the organization's priorities? What would be the most disruptive obstacle to achieving success with each of them? What would keep them from developing the way that they were planned? Start small. Don't pick all the priorities—just pick some of the important ones.

Changing the way you and your organization think and behave takes time. It has to be centered on something that is cared about. We do what we care about. What do you want to accomplish? What does that picture of success look like? Like culture, this will be unique for your organization. What potential unplanned event could be the most disruptive to you or your organization?

Why do people balance checkbooks? They want to know how much money they have in their checking accounts. They don't want to run out of funds—or they are saving for something and are trying to accumulate enough funds to purchase it. Some people don't balance their checkbooks because they know they have enough money to cover their bills on a monthly basis. They know they will always have a positive balance and are not concerned with what the balance is. Those who balance their checkbooks proactively take certain actions. For those who manually do it, they periodically balance the checkbook against a financial statement. For those who automatically do it, they periodically validate the calculation. Both typically have a running balance of the funds available and look at it frequently.

For those who are concerned about paying the bills, a significant unplanned event would be forgetting to. For those saving for something, the unplanned event would be trying to buy what they wanted without the funds—or having the funds and not making the purchase. If they didn't proactively keep track of the balance, they would never know what they have. Because they care about it, they proactively are involved with the balance. As a result, they are applying all five behaviors that lead to LeadeReliability and are minimizing any impact of an unplanned event. They are proactively looking at information to make sure there are no unplanned events. This same mentality can be applied to anything we care about.

What are the indications that things are normal? More importantly, what would be the earliest sign of abnormality? What is the indication that something is wrong? What will you notice that has become different from normal? Is it a behavior, a measurement, an electronic indication, or a sound? Could it be even more subtle—like a comment, an action, or a nonaction? What will be the first indication that your plans will be disrupted? When you have identified it, put a system in place to monitor that indication proactively rather than reactively. Notice when it happens—and take predetermined actions to minimize the impact. Being proactive and doing something will minimize the disruption—and may even prevent anything from going wrong.

An unplanned event usually gets the attention of an organization. In most organizations that have not thought about

LeadeReliability, the resolution to the issue is started after the disruption has taken place. The unplanned event typically is disruptive enough that an investigation to find out what happened is started. Since what happened usually is negative, an effort is made by the organization to figure out why it occurred.

Here are some examples of what it could be for an organization:

- an injury to one of the employees
- a lost customer
- a mistake that causes a large amount of products to be rejected or thrown away
- a mistake that has significant financial implications
- a split of the organization into factions
- an ended relationship

In these significant events, what actions are taken? The organization tries to discover what went wrong and looks for how it happened. This process is often referred to as a root cause investigation or a root cause analysis, but the premise is to simply understand how it happened.

The process typically begins by going back to determine which triggering mechanism started the chain of events that caused the disruption or unplanned event. The level and thoroughness to which this analysis takes place will ultimately determine if there are actions that can be taken to prevent the incident from happening again. Some organizations are better than others at doing this, but it is not enough.

In most cases, this process will lead to a series of actions aimed at preventing a reoccurrence of the event. Ideally this will be aimed broadly throughout the organization, but in my experience, it is not always successful. A measure of the success of this approach is to think about how many repeat unplanned events occur. Most organizations regularly have repeat or duplicate unplanned events.

Why doesn't the approach that is described above lead to a systemic solution for preventing a repeat event—even though that is the intention? Why does it fall short? The system of finding the root cause of the event is a great system for understanding the incident, but since it is reactive and has a narrow focus, it always happens after the event. Often finding the root cause becomes the point of success of the investigation, the learning—and not necessarily in preventing it from happening again, the teaching. In most organizations, significant time is taken to uncover the root cause, but unless the event was extremely disruptive, not nearly as much time was spent on preventing reoccurrences.

LeadeReliability requires that we minimize the impact of unplanned events. In order to do that once we see something abnormal, we have to decide to do something and then act. Unlike the process described above, when you are LeadeReliable, any time an unplanned event does occur, it has to be thoroughly understood and actions taken so that it never happens again, which requires us to "learn and teach." These two actions of leadership must be performed to minimize the impact of unplanned events and ensure those that do occur are never repeated. In order for the organization to become LeadeReliable, the entire organization must become leaders—doing something, learning, and teaching when the opportunities arise.

ELIMINATE REPETITIVE UNPLANNED EVENTS THROUGH REACTIVE ACTIONS.

Although the proactive approach is the most effective, it is foreign to organizations. In a reactive case, a completely disruptive event makes your organization go through the effort of understanding the root cause.

If you have not uncovered human behaviors and management systems that have contributed to the unplanned events, you haven't dug deep enough. If your root cause analysis ends with something mechanical or electrical or physical that happened, you have not thoroughly investigated why. If something failed, there was a human behavior or management system in almost all cases that caused it to fail. Many times that behavior—induced by a known or unknown management system—was the root cause and the reason for the failure.

Whatever you have decided on for your root cause, determine the first indication that had occurred that caused the unplanned event to happen. What were the early signs? What was the birth of abnormal? If you don't know, start asking why—and use history to discover the first indication. If you think you know, ask yourself if there was an earlier indication of the occurrence.

Here is a simple example on how each situation works, but your response will dictate whether you are LeadeReliable. In the example below, the outcome could have been much different, but it ended up being an unplanned event.

On your way to an appointment, you find yourself stranded beside the road with a flat right rear tire. By the time you change the spare, you will be late. This is a significant unplanned event because you will now miss the appointment that took you three months to schedule.

As you change the tire, you think about how you could have been so unlucky—but were you unlucky or unreliable?

When you were having the oil changed three weeks earlier, the service manager said they always check the tire pressure of all the cars they work on as a customer service and put a little air in your right rear tire. The service manager encouraged you to keep an eye on that. You thanked her and thought nothing more about it.

Days later, you got a signal that your right rear tire pressure was low. You convinced yourself that it was because it was the first cold morning of the fall. The warning light didn't come on the next day. About a week ago, your neighbor said it looked like your right rear tire was a little low. You thanked him for the information—but decided it wasn't that bad. Besides, the tire air pressure indication warning wasn't always on.

Yesterday, your wife heard a little squealing sound from the rear of your car—and the warning light was on. As you were leaving the garage to head for your appointment, you noticed the warning light again. As you drove, the car seemed to be handling a little funny. At the last traffic light, the person beside you seemed to be trying to get your attention, but you ignored her.

If you had reacted to any of these early indications, you may have been able to put air in your tire, take the car to have the tire inspected, or put some instant flat-tire repair into your tire. As you are removing the spare tire and jack from the car, some of these early indications flash through your mind. All these were early indications that something was wrong with your right rear tire. Was the dealer's comment the first warning? It may have been, but was there an earlier indication that something could be wrong. At a construction site about a month ago, you noticed a few nails on the ground. You thought, *I sure hope I don't get one of these in my tire.*

If you were LeadeReliable, you would have used all five behaviors to anticipate a potential problem and would have inspected the tire at the first indication that there was something wrong. Someone who is not LeadeReliable would be on the side of the road missing an important appointment.

When you noticed the nails, you used resilience, deference to expertise, and sensitivity to operations to say the nails on the ground near my car are not a good thing and could cause a problem. However, you failed to use the behavior (reluctance to simplify) because had you been reluctant to simplify, any future indication of a tire problem should have caused you to believe (using preoccupation with failure) that you potentially had a nail in your tire. Instead, you didn't practice these two behaviors—and you are on the side of the road.

How does leadership come into play? Leaders say, "I need to do something." You left the nails on the ground and didn't pick them up. If you had, maybe you would have prevented your own flat tire. Also, you didn't tell anyone about them. How many other damaged tires resulted from the spilled nails?

What about the leadership at the construction site? Someone dropped those nails. How many others saw the nails and didn't do anything about them. Immediately after the nails were dropped, there were many opportunities for you not to have had a flat tire.

It starts with the personal reliability of every person involved. You could have done more about your own situation—but so could others have. The person who dropped the nails could have done more. Anyone at the construction site who saw the nails could have done more. You could have done more—a number of times. The auto mechanic could have done more. Your neighbor could have done more. Your wife could have done more. Even the person at the traffic light could have done more. Personal reliability leads to organizational reliability, and organizational reliability gives birth to personal reliability. Instead, lack of both has left you stranded.

Apply this example to how things work for you or your organization. Multiple times each day—in most organizations—the first indication that something could go wrong goes unnoticed. The proactive response is to think about what kinds of things are disruptive to you or your organization. Identify the top five things initially. Before they occur, determine the earliest indications that those disruptions could be starting. What has to happen before the disruption can occur? Instead of waiting until after the disruption, look proactively for that early indication to occur. Look at it with a frequency that will cause you to discover it early—and then train yourself to understand what you can do to correct the situation—and then do it. If you take that action, the disruption can never occur for that reason. This process will cause you to examine things early and catch them early too.

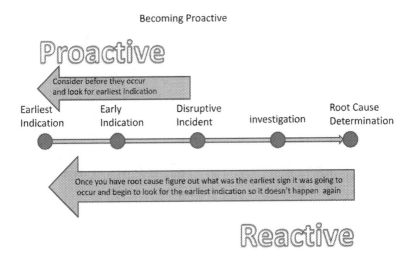

Becoming Proactive

Now you have started the proactive approach, but you won't be perfect. You are now looking at a set of early indications for the top disruptions, but others will occur because you are early in the process. Put on your reactive hat and go to work. Instead of addressing the one incident through a series of independent action items, take a systemic approach to solving the problem. Identify the earliest sign that what occurred was going to occur and add that indication to your list.

Now you will be proactively looking at the major indications from the incident. Each time you have an incident, add to the list. Three things will happen if you have committed to addressing the early indications as soon as they happen and resolving them.

- The significant disruption will not occur unless there is another way it can occur that you are not looking at. If there is, you will discover it in the reactive approach—and that will only happen once.

- You will not have repeat incidents because the incidents that occur are systemically addressed instead of individually.
- The organization will suggest other things that they are aware of that should be looked at proactively.

As a result, you will see a reduction in unplanned events—and you will minimize the impact of any that do occur.

You may ask how there will be time to proactively look at all these early indications, since one of the issues raised before was lack of time and resources. If you have the early indication identified—and it is measurable, recognizable, or detectable—you are only looking for abnormal. If it is normal, there is no action required—and you can move on. If it is abnormal, you must commit to addressing it. Early on, you will want to ignore the early indication (not practicing preoccupation with failure) or you will try to explain it away (not practicing reluctance to simplify), but commit to yourself that you will understand why the early indication occurred and correct it. Once corrected, the impact will be minor or none.

Since the process was started small—and at the beginning—the number of observations will not be overwhelming. Since only the abnormal is being addressed, the process is not time-consuming. As other issues are detected early and resolved, the number of unplanned events begins to be reduced, which frees up time to discover even more issues to proactively observe. With increased practice in the process, the abnormal will be detected early and addressed before it is disruptive. The process will become contagious and will become one of the biggest ways that you will continue to capture hearts.

Think about what happens when you have an unplanned event. You spend hours—if not days—and significant economic resources in a reactive manner to resolve the issue. With this approach, you are spending much less time and many fewer resources to proactively resolve issues.

Getting to Do What You Planned on Doing

This is the reward of starting the journey toward LeadeReliability. Time and resources are being utilized in a planned fashion toward individual and organizational success. Significant waste caused by unplanned events is being eliminated.

The individual has time to think, plan, learn, teach, and accomplish what he or she planned on doing. The job—and life in general—is becoming much more enjoyable. The organization is becoming more dependable, reliable, successful, and profitable.

The culture is changing.

CHAPTER 11

Ways to Monitor, Evaluate, and Sustain Progress

Any knowledge that doesn't lead to new questions quickly dies out.
—Wislawa Szymborska

You have started to see the culture move, and you are beginning to see results. Depending on how widespread the success and how large the organization is, this is a good start, but most organizations fail because of a lack of patience.

What does it take to create success? To ensure that the culture continues to progress toward LeadeReliability, these are some of the things that can continue your forward movement.

- Listen for the stories of how people are minimizing unplanned events and share those stories with others.
- Constantly create awareness about the desire to minimize unplanned events and talk about it all the time.
- The culture is changing one person at a time, so become extremely patient about making sustainable progress.
- Celebrate each success.

- Reward and recognize those who are proactively minimizing unplanned events and expect the performance of reactively dealing with unplanned events.
- Insist that unplanned events are not repeated, and work at proactively identifying the initial causes.

The first indication that a heart has changed and a person is focused on LeadeReliability is that they will talk about minimizing unplanned events. Their words and behaviors will minimize the impact of unplanned events. They will become much more reliable. They will talk with others about becoming reliable and say that they need to do something about it. They will share their thoughts and ideas with others.

Awareness about becoming more reliable can never take a rest. Constant awareness is the energy in the process. The definition of constantly and consistently keeping your commitments never stops. It has to be talked about all the time. Once the heart is committed, that person will never stop. Going back is just too painful. As more people develop reasons to care about minimizing the impact of unplanned events, they continue to raise awareness with others.

There is a snowball effect with LeadeReliability. As people have success and increase the frequency in which they get to do what they planned on doing, they enjoy the benefits. Instead of unplanned events being treated as normal, they are treated as an affront to the culture. People attempt to solve the unplanned event and minimize its impact, and they go out of their way to learn from it, share their learning, and ensure that the fundamental systemic issue is addressed so that unplanned events never happen again.

Culture change is hard work and requires patience, which is a trait that most people have trouble displaying. Organizations lack patience too. With so many organizational pressures, organizational patience is hard to achieve. This lack of patience is a major cause that derails LeadeReliability. As the culture is developing, the journey requires significant activation energy to start—and it takes a while before measurable gains are made. Immediate significant results are not like a switch that you can turn on, but there are often pressures and expectations for them. Especially from those who don't understand the requirements necessary to achieve LeadeReliability. The impatience begins to detract from celebrating early progress and draws focus on the lack of fast results. This focus on the negative becomes a major source of distraction. When this impatience surfaces—and it most likely will—what will you do about it? The moment that any distraction takes over as the point of focus, LeadeReliability has begun to stop advancing.

Persistent patience with results is needed to drive LeadeReliability. The reason you started the journey in the first place was because the old culture was delivering insufficient results, but behavioral change takes time. Being patient and celebrating the small successes is necessary. Every unplanned event that is minimized is part of the journey and may be the reason another heart gets captured. This cultural change process will have occurred one person at a time. For some, the reason to change will come quickly, but others need time to figure out why they care. If everyone could magically be changed at once, many organizations would have this culture. Only a few have continued the journey far enough to be on their way to LeadeReliability, but they have created a culture that will differentiate the organization from most, if not all, of their competition.

So if immediate significant short-term results with no sustainability are more important to you than lasting and differentiating performance, then LeadeReliability will not work for you. But if you want to create an organization that outperforms its competition and thrills its customers, stakeholders, and employees, then LeadeReliability is the answer because new success will be created each time a person develops a reason to care.

Success needs to be the constant focus—and not the speed of success. Examples of success can be used continuously; actions taken, shared knowledge, and constant teachings are the tools that capture hearts. Focus on individual and group successes. Each time someone successfully takes action to minimize the impact of an unplanned event, celebrate it—and share it with others. Translate these successes into stories that demonstrate for the organization how the desired behaviors work to minimize the impact of unplanned events and the value that is created. These examples and stories can be used as a living history of what success looks like and how impactful the behaviors can be. Every organization is different, so putting the desired behaviors into the organization's words and examples will allow others in the organization to understand what is meant by LeadeReliability.

Reward those who take proactive behavior to minimize the impact of unplanned events—and stop rewarding the firefighters and rescuers who come in after the unplanned event has taken its toll. People tend to duplicate the actions and behaviors that are most rewarded. If someone proactively solves a problem, once it is known, teach the learning and reward the behavior. Make it known that you want to know about proactive resolution of problems so that those behaviors can be rewarded. Stop rewarding those who correct problems after the fact. Although it is typically good work, since the unplanned event already took its toll, the resources are already wasted—and the damage has already occurred.

No matter when the unplanned event is discovered, the impact of the outcome can always be minimized—and those behaviors should be rewarded. It is important to investigate all unplanned events, whether they are proactively or reactively resolved, but it is critical that the behaviors that proactively solve the problems are rewarded.

Repeat unplanned events happen all the time and are considered normal in a nonreliable culture. As disruptive unplanned events are analyzed, ask if a similar unplanned event has happened before. In many cases, it has happened within two years of the most recent occurrence.

The reason that organizations have repeat unplanned events is the failure to teach. The only way to learn is to learn for ourselves or be taught by others. If the latter is not happening, then each person has to learn everything for themselves. This leads to a lot of unplanned events that could have been avoided. It is easy to see why unplanned events are repeated, if the resolution is always targeted individually and never a systemic approach. How can they be stopped? Address the systemic reason for the unplanned event to stop it from occurring again. Attempting to address them from outside of the management system limits the learning and makes it harder to share the results with others.

Typically one management system and one action within the system will eliminate the repeat of the event, not only for the specific failure but for all similar ones across the system. Here is an example: if a piece of equipment failed because vibration during its operation got so severe that the failure was catastrophic, the option is to focus on that one piece of equipment or to broaden the view and focus on all similar pieces of equipment throughout the system. If you focus on the one piece of equipment, you will solve the one problem, but it could happen again someplace else in the system. If you focus the solution system wide on all similar pieces of equipment, you will solve the problem systematically and minimize many future unplanned events. The benefit is widespread and is not targeted to the one piece of equipment that failed but to all equipment that could fail in the future that way. Done this way, all like pieces of equipment will never catastrophically fail because of high vibration; one system with one action proactively taken, not multiple actions items directed at the one piece of equipment. Teaching how to prevent them from happening by being proactive is the only way to reduce and potentially eliminate unplanned events from happening again.

As you see cultural movement and individuals changing their behaviors, you must be adamant about your focus on unplanned events. Your expectation must be that you minimize the impact of the unplanned event before it happens; if unplanned events do happen, you never allow them to repeat themselves.

Every unplanned event you minimize the impact of allows you to do what you planned on doing and allows you to use the resources to create profit, customer loyalty, and employee satisfaction. By constantly monitoring your progress, listening for these indications, and taking these actions, the journey will continue.

CHAPTER 12

AN EVERGREEN AND EVER-EVOLVING CULTURE

The great thing in the world is not so much where
we stand, as in what direction we are moving.
—Oliver Wendell Holmes

D o you ever achieve a culture that constantly and completely meets all of its commitments? Are you ever as reliable as you could be? Are you ever as reliable as you should be? Are you able to stop and be satisfied with the reliability you have achieved?

The answer to all these questions is no. This is a continuous journey that really never ends. The moment you drive toward LeadeReliability is the moment you start a journey that can always be refined. Most individuals and organizations have many levels of unreliability; you can always peel the onion and get a little better. Don't be discouraged by this. The fact that the journey is never finished does not mean it won't have significant results along the way. There will be noticeable results and many instances to celebrate. Because the journey is long, those results may not be realized until a comparison is made with where the journey started. Others from the outside may notice it before those in the organization do. They will notice the change quicker because they are not involved with the change every day.

The significance of the journey will be on professional and personal levels. It will have a positive impact on the organization and a tremendous impact on those outside the organization. Customers will no longer wonder if they will get their products or if they will be on time. Employees will enjoy coming to work and will get to do what they planned on doing because they know that their days will not be interrupted. Individuals will find the time to think and plan—rather than always doing. They will have time to consider and contemplate rather than always reacting. The bottom line will incrementally and then significantly improve.

Since much of what is being done is preventing negative things from happening by minimizing the impact of unplanned events, a significant cost benefit will occur. The cost of getting work done will be lower because employees are no longer duplicating efforts by redoing or reworking things. The work that never seems to get done will get done. Activities are planned more frequently and accomplished as planned. Individuals have the time to watch for small deviations that may occur—and have planned what they will do if they do. They have taken the time to analyze past learning and to talk to experts before undertaking the task.

When small things that could derail an activity occur, they are noticed and addressed because they have been preidentified as possible issues. Activities and projects are successfully accomplished in the least amount of time possible. Analysis is performed on all activities to glean learning and knowledge so they can be applied to the next time the activity is done. This knowledge is shared with others who may benefit from it so others don't have to learn for themselves.

LeadeReliability is the only thing I know that creates time. When others become excited about what they are doing—and they minimize the impact of unplanned events—they accomplish what they have planned on doing because unplanned events don't disrupt those plans. This creates time to evaluate how they or someone else can do what needs to be done even more efficiently, which creates time to do other things.

Necessity is the mother of invention, but a strong ally to invention is having time to think. Becoming an organization that constantly and consistently meets its commitments gives the organization flexibility to grow if desired, increased profits and margins, and creates time to invent and innovate. Invention and innovation require time to think, plan, consider, and contemplate—and then the resources and time to try it out. If there is always a state of reaction going on and resources are spent redoing things that didn't work the first time, then time is never spent moving forward. Instead it is spent catching up.

Organizations that are not LeadeReliable are always trying to figure out what they are, and they never have the chance to figure out what they could be. Unplanned events dictate how time will be used. Early in the journey, unplanned events prevent any chance of continually meeting commitments and any chance for innovation. This begins to change as the organization sticks to the journey.

If performing to full potential is the desire, then LeadeReliability is how everything gets done. It allows the organization and individuals to constantly and consistently meet their commitments. Organizations work hard at how they do things—and not always at what they do. What they do sometimes requires thought, patience, and planning—and very little action. Although they are always progressing, they could appear not to be busy. From the outside, one might describe what they see as control rather than chaos. From the inside, vigilant is probably a better description.

LeadeReliable organizations are on a constant journey of improvement and understand how they can do things better with less waste. They are easily identified because every individual in the organization has developed a reason to care about constantly and consistently meeting commitments—and he or she can describe what that is. The organization is passionate about what it does, but employees will first tell you why they do it. They are not immune to distraction, but distraction never becomes the focus. It simply becomes another reason to become LeadeReliable. Leadership is apparent throughout the organization; no matter the situation, individuals take action to ensure the impact of any unplanned event is mitigated.

Can a brand ever be too good? Can a customer ever be too satisfied? Can a stakeholder ever be too happy with performance? Can there ever be too much time to think? Again the answer is no, but in this case, no is a very good thing. Leadership is practiced throughout the organization. If this sounds too good to be true, when you live it, it will seem like it is. Not many achieve it, but those that do become highly successful. The organization is respected because commitments are met and people usually get to do what they planned on doing. When they don't, they use the opportunity to improve even more.

Warren Bennis said (*italics mine*), "A leader is one who manifests direction (*alignment*), integrity (*meeting commitments*), hardiness (*willingness to persevere*), and courage in a consistent pattern of behavior (*the five behaviors we have discussed*) that inspires trust, motivation (*sparks interest in minimizing the impact of unplanned events*), and responsibility (*I need to do something*) on the part of followers (*those who academically agree*) who in turn become leaders themselves (*a personal reason to care*)."

Take the journey and stick with it—and every part of your personal and professional life will change positively. It is hard work. There will be resistance—you can count on it. But if you continue to move forward, you will create something that not many people achieve. As a result, you will set yourself apart from most others—you will be LeadeReliable.

We end the journey with the same question we started with. Why reliability? You have discovered the answer. LeadeReliability is not what you do—but how you do everything. You have always known what to do to be successful, but now you can change how you do it and become successful. LeadeReliability allows you to do your work in a way that ensures success and self-satisfaction. You will become a person who constantly and consistently delivers on all of your commitments.

It is your choice to decide whether to take your first step toward LeadeReliability. If you do, you will create a world where you get to do what you planned on doing for a day, a week, a month, a year, and more.

SUGGESTED READING

At Canaan's Edge, Taylor Branch
1864: Lincoln at the Gates of History, Charles Bracelen Floods
Good to Great, Jim Collins
Leadership and Self-Deception, The Arbinger Institute
Lone Survivor, Marcus Luttrell with Patrick Robinson
Long Walk to Freedom, Nelson Mandela
Managing the Unexpected, Karl Weick and Kathleen Sutcliffe
Speed of Trust, Stephen M. R. Covey
Start with Why: How Great Leaders Inspire Everyone to Take Action,
    Simon Sinek
The 21 Irrefutable Laws of Leadership, John C. Maxwell
Unbroken, Laura Hillenbrand
Up from Slavery, Booker T. Washington

REFERENCES

Atlanta Journal Constitution, www.AJC.com, December 12, 2012.

DAL stock price, May 15, 2013.

CarMD.com 2010 Vehicle Health Index, 5 Most Common Failures.

CarMD.com 2010 Vehicle Health Index, 5 Most Common Failures

Deming, W. Edwards. *Out of the Crisis: Quality, Productivity, and Competitive Position.* Cambridge: Cambridge University Press, 1982.

"History of Delta," www.delta.com.

Juran.com, "Juran: The Source of Quality," article on the founder.

Kutless. "What Faith Can Do." *All Is Well: A Worship Album.* 2009.

McNair, Sam. "Budgeting for Maintenance: A Behavior-Based Approach." <http://www.plantservices.com/wp_downloads/pdf/110912-Life-Cycle-Engineering-budgeting-maintenance.pdf>

Money.cnn.com\magazine\Fortune 500. 2012 List.

Sinek, Simon. *Start with Why: How Great Leaders Inspire Everyone to Take Action.* New York, New York: Penguin Books, 2009.

"Total Recall: Impact Assessment of Toyota's Quality Issues on Its North American Business," February 17, 2010.

Weick, Karl E., and Kathleen Sutcliffe. *Managing the Unexpected.* San Francisco, CA: John Wiley & Sons, 2007.

Yahoo AP report, December 14, 2011.

Yahoo AP report, December 12, 2012.